The Ocean of Story

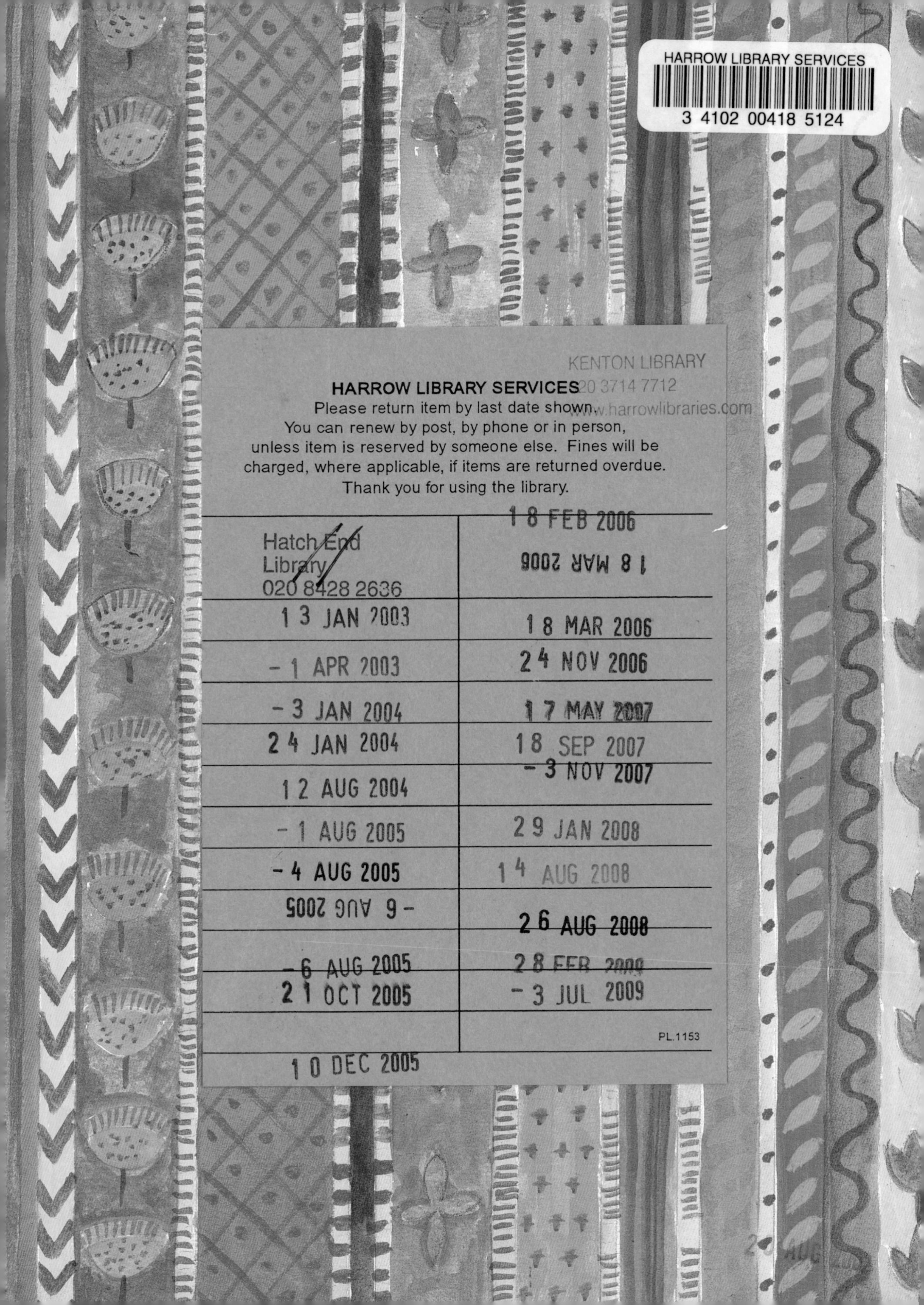
HARROW LIBRARY SERVICES
3 4102 00418 5124
KENTON LIBRARY
020 3714 7712
www.harrowlibraries.com
HARROW LIBRARY SERVICES
Please return item by last date shown.
You can renew by post, by phone or in person,
unless item is reserved by someone else. Fines will be
charged, where applicable, if items are returned overdue.
Thank you for using the library.
Hatch End
Library
020 8428 2636
13 JAN 2003
- 1 APR 2003
- 3 JAN 2004
24 JAN 2004
12 AUG 2004
- 1 AUG 2005
- 4 AUG 2005
- 6 AUG 2005
- 6 AUG 2005
21 OCT 2005
10 DEC 2005
18 FEB 2006
18 MAR 2006
18 MAR 2006
24 NOV 2006
17 MAY 2007
18 SEP 2007
- 3 NOV 2007
29 JAN 2008
14 AUG 2008
26 AUG 2008
- 3 JUL 2009
PL.1153

THE OCEAN OF STORY

· A Collection of Magical Folk Tales ·

Chosen with an Introduction
and Notes by Neil Philip

RETOLD BY CAROLINE NESS

Illustrated by Jacqueline Mair

MACDONALD YOUNG BOOKS

For Emma and Neil
for one thousand and one reasons
C.N.

In memory of Jimmie Dinwiddie
who gave me my first chance to love India,
and for Bula Chakravarty Agbo
a lifelong friend I made when I got there
J.M.

Conceived, designed and produced by
The Albion Press Ltd, Spring Hill, Idbury, Oxfordshire OX7 6RU

Designer: Emma Bradford
Project Manager: Elizabeth Wilkes

First published in Great Britain in 1995 by Macdonald Young Books
Campus 400, Maylands Avenue, Hemel Hempstead, Herts HP2 7EZ

1 3 5 7 9 10 8 6 4 2

ISBN 0–7500–1688–4

A CIP catalogue record for this book is available from the British Library

Typesetting by York House Typographic Ltd, London
Colour origination by York House Graphics Ltd, London
Printed in Hong Kong

Contents

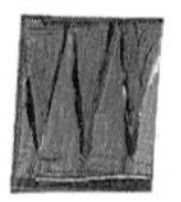

Introduction

THE INDIAN SUB-CONTINENT is unusual in having both a classical and a popular folktale tradition. The classical, Sanskrit, tradition, embraces such literary collections as the *Jatakas* (which tell of the previous incarnations of the Buddha), the fables of the *Panchatantra*, the involved narratives of the *Kathá Sarit Ságara* ("The Ocean of the Streams of Story"), and the great epics of the *Ramayana* and the *Mahabharata*. The popular tradition consists, in the words of Lal Behari Day, of the tales "which old women in India recite to little children in the evening."

Yet these two traditions are essentially the same. Modern Indians still tell stories found in the *Panchatantra*, which was compiled around the fifth century AD by Vishnusarman; the *Panchatantra* itself was incorporated in the *Kathá Sarit Ságara*, compiled by Somadeva in the twelfth century; village versions of many of Somadeva's stories can still be heard.

Because all the stories of India, whether written or oral, seem to flow into one another, it has seemed right to borrow Somadeva's title, *The Ocean of Story*, for this collection, which is mostly made up of tales collected from oral tradition at the end of the last century. Some of these stories, such as "Kanai the Gardener," can also be found in the original work, and three of them, including "Three Fussy Men," have been taken from it.

"Three Fussy Men" leads us to another fascinating area of study: in it we have a twelfth-century Sanskrit variant of a story now famous in a nineteenth-century Danish literary version, Hans Christian Andersen's "The Princess and the Pea." Other stories remind us of similar tales in Aesop, or Uncle Remus, or Grimm. India's ocean of story has encircled the world.

Yet though we can recognize many similarities with Western fairy tales, the stories in this book are deeply rooted in Indian culture. They are profoundly concerned, for instance, with questions of fate and destiny, and correspondingly less concerned with happy endings and just rewards. Anecdotes and fables about cleverness and folly, tricksters and gulls, are popular; so too are long, rambling wonder tales in which the richness comes from narrative embellishment rather than structural economy. The stories-within-stories of a tale such as "The Wonderful Ring" are typical, and remind us that Somadeva's *Ocean of Story* is to all intents and purposes the Indian equivalent of the *Arabian Nights*.

The extent to which seemingly familiar stories take their own distinct shape in India might be seen in the Cinderella variant in this book, "The Boy and his Stepmother." Collected from the Santal tribes of northern India, it has both a male "Cinderella" and an unhappy ending, and the Cinderella figure loses a hair from his head, not a shoe.

The Indian sub-continent is home to over a hundred living languages and countless dialects. Its cultures and folk traditions are immeasurably old, and anything one says about them must be a simplification. But there is, surely, something simple and universal about storytelling. Across any distance of time, space, or culture, everyone can recognize the childhood memories of Anna Liberata de Souza, from whom this book's "The Brahman, the Tiger, and the Six Judges" was originally recorded:

"No sooner my granny's back turned than we all ran out in the sun and played with the dust and stones on the road. Then my granny would call out to us, 'Come here, children, out of the sun, and I'll tell you a story. Come in, you'll all get headaches.' So she used to get us together (there were nine of us, and great little fidgets, like all children) into the house; and there she'd sit on the floor, and tell us one of the stories I tell you. But then she used to make them last much longer, the different people telling their own stories from the beginning as often as possible; so that by the time she'd got to the end she had told the beginning over five or six times. And so she went on, talk, talk, talk, *Mera Bapreh!* [O, my father!] such a long time she'd go on for, till all the children got quite tired and fell asleep."

Neil Philip

The Cat Who Became a Queen

MANY YEARS AGO there was a king who had hundreds of wives but no children. Eventually this became too much for him to bear. He stormed around the palace in a terrible temper, his face tight, his fists clenched.

"Why me?" he roared. "What have I done to deserve this? What is wrong with these women? Hundreds of wives and not a single child! Well, I've been patient long enough! If one of them does not produce a child within the next year, I'll banish the lot of them and start again!"

The harem was thrown into a frenzy. Every wife prayed that she would bear the king's child, but as the months slipped by it became obvious that none of them were pregnant.

Fearful of banishment, they sent word to the king that one of his wives was expecting a child, and in due course they announced the birth of a princess. In actual fact, the harem cat had had a litter of kittens and the king's wives had adopted one of them. Naturally, the proud father asked to see his daughter, but the wives had anticipated this request and sent word that the Brahman had declared that the child must not be seen by her father until her wedding day.

The years went by and the king constantly inquired tenderly after his daughter. He had longed for a son to succeed him, but he was content. By all accounts, his daughter was wise, healthy, and beautiful: he would marry her to a suitable prince and she would make him proud.

When his daughter was old enough to marry, the king sent for his councillors and instructed them to find a prince worthy of her. Eventually a handsome, clever, and kind-hearted prince was found and the marriage was arranged. What on earth were the king's wives to do now? Surely they would be found out? They put their heads together and decided that there was nothing for it but to confide in the prince and trust to his good nature not to betray them. So they sent for the prince and told him everything, making him swear not to reveal their secret to anyone, not even his own family.

The marriage was a lavish affair, lasting all day and most of the night. The king, having eaten and drunk rather more than was good for him, let the wedding party go without seeing his daughter. If he had looked in the carriage, he would have found a cat sitting on a silk cushion.

The wedding party reached the prince's country safely, and the prince smuggled his wife into his room without anyone seeing. He took great care of the cat, showering her with love and affection, but he made sure that the room was locked at all times and forbade anyone to enter.

One day while the prince was away, his mother went up to his room and knocked on the door, saying, "My dear daughter-in-law, I just wanted to tell you how sorry I am that you are locked in this room all the time and forbidden to see anyone. It must be so lonely for you. I long to meet you, my dear, but perhaps you do not wish to meet me. I am going out today — you could leave your room and no one would see you. Will you come out?"

The cat understood every word. Realizing that she was condemned to her lonely existence forever, she wept bitterly, thinking of the long years ahead. The sound of her crying was so heartrending that the prince's mother, herself upset, vowed that she would give her son a piece of her mind on his return. But Pavarti, wife of the great god Shiva, also heard the cat and rushed to Shiva, begging him to have mercy on the poor, helpless cat.

"Tell her," said Shiva, "that there is a small bottle of orange blossom oil in her room. She must rub it all over her body. Her fur will vanish and she will become a beautiful woman."

As soon as the cat was told this, she rubbed the oil all over herself, leaving one tiny patch of fur on her left shoulder so that her husband would believe her incredible story and recognize her as his wife.

When the prince returned that evening, he found the most breathtakingly beautiful woman in his room. When he learned that she was his wife, he was overjoyed and wasted no time in introducing her to his family. His mother took one look at the radiantly happy girl and saw there was no need to scold her son. This, surely, was a marriage made in heaven.

A few weeks later the prince and his wife visited his father-in-law. The king, seeing his daughter for the first time, was quite overcome by her beauty, but no more so than his wives, who, much to the king's surprise, were struck dumb. The king made the prince his heir, and in due course the prince became king of both countries and the cat was his queen.

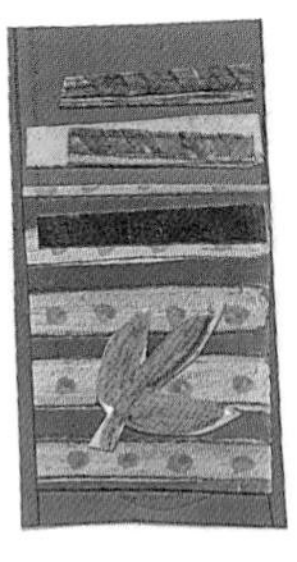

Kanai the Gardener

KANAI, THE RAJAH'S GARDENER, had the greenest fingers in the kingdom. He talked as he worked, and the plants seemed to thrive on his voice and touch. Trees, shrubs, and flowers had been brought from every corner of the globe, and each one, tended by Kanai, grew to twice its usual size. Frangipani, roses, lotus flowers, lilies; the garden was a bright, fragrant paradise. There was just one puzzle that Kanai had yet to solve: each night, the choicest fruits in the garden were eaten by some mysterious creature.

Kanai usually left the garden at dusk, but one night he had had more work to do than usual and it was almost midnight before he thought about going home. The earthy smell of evening still hung in the air, but the moon was full, and sharp fingers of light lit the silent garden. Suddenly the peace was broken by a tremendous crash. The earth seemed to shift underfoot and the trees bent and groaned. Terrified, Kanai hid behind a tree.

An enormous elephant came down from the sky and into the garden. After much thought, Kanai realized that this could only be Oirabot, the heavenly elephant, and he was determined to follow it and see where it went and what it did. Kanai shadowed Oirabot as he roamed around the garden, pulling up the tenderest shoots and plucking the ripest fruit from the trees. He couldn't help noticing that despite the elephant's enormous size, the garden was not damaged in any way.

When the elephant had finally eaten its fill and looked as if it was about to leave, Kanai grasped its tail and clung on grimly. Oirabot began to soar upward, oblivious of his passenger.

As soon as they arrived in heaven, Kanai let go of Oirabot's tail. Everything was so huge, much bigger than in the Rajah's garden even! Enormous mangoes, tea plantations like forests, cows as big as elephants, and elephants the size of houses! And everything was so cheap! Kanai bought a mango and a betel nut to show his wife, then gorged himself until sunset. Some time later, his stomach tight and his head heavy, he found Oirabot and sat down beside him to wait until he made his journey back to earth.

That night Oirabot returned to the garden for his midnight feast with Kanai clinging onto his tail. As soon as they were on firm ground, Kanai loosened his grip and hurried home to his wife. She was beside herself with worry, since her husband was usually reliable and she had not seen him for two whole days.

"Where on earth have you been? I asked everyone I could think of if they had seen you, but no one had!"

Without saying a word, Kanai handed her the mango and the betel nut. When she saw them, his wife danced around with excitement.

"Where did you get them? Where did you get them?"

Kanai told her all about his adventures and how cheap and plentiful food was in heaven.

"I want to go too! Take me with you tonight!" said his wife.

"All right! All right! But whatever you do, don't tell anyone else about this. It must be our secret."

"I wouldn't dream of telling anyone else," his wife retorted.

Later that afternoon, Kanai's wife went to the well to fetch some water. Her best friend was there.

"It won't hurt to tell my best friend," thought Kanai's wife.

So, swearing her to secrecy, she told her friend the whole story.

Well, that friend told *her* best friend and she in turn told *her* best friend, who told her husband, who told his brother, and soon everyone in the town had heard the story. They all arrived at Kanai's house demanding to be taken to heaven. What could Kanai do? He had to agree. Everyone flocked to the garden to wait for Oirabot. When the elephant appeared, Kanai said, "This is what we'll do. As Oirabot is about to leave, I'll grab his tail with one hand, then my wife will hold my other hand, her friend will hold on to her, and so on. That way, we'll all get to heaven."

When Oirabot showed signs of leaving, Kanai seized his tail and they all formed a chain, as agreed. The elephant climbed higher and higher. He was almost past the seventieth star when Kanai's wife's best friend asked, "How big was the betel nut your husband brought home?"

Kanai's wife repeated the question to her husband. "Just wait and see!" he replied.

"That's not good enough! She wants to know now!" said Kanai's wife.

Kanai, utterly exasperated, said, "They were about this big." As he spoke, he let go of the elephant's tail and stretched his hands out to show the size, and Kanai, with his wife and all their friends, tumbled head over heels back down to earth.

The Wind and the Sun

THE WIND AND THE SUN were arguing as to which was the stronger.

"I am more powerful than you," said the Sun.

"No you're not," said the Wind. "I am stronger, and I'll prove it! You see that man over there with a cloak around his shoulders? I bet you I can tear it off him quicker than you can."

"Done!" said the Sun.

The Wind tried first. It blew up a storm. It blew up a gale. It blew so hard that the man was almost swept off his feet, but he tied his cloak tightly around him and leaned into the blast. Finally the Wind gave up.

"You have a go!" he said to the Sun.

The Sun rose. Round, red, and brilliant, it blazed down mercilessly. The man began to sweat. The sweat rolled down his face and onto his neck and shoulders, and he began to feel very uncomfortable. Puffing with exertion, the man took off his cloak to cool down.

The Wind, defeated, blew away.

The King and his Daughters

THERE WAS ONCE A KING who had three daughters. He began to worry which daughter loved him best, so he called them to him.

"How much do you love me?" he asked the first.

"As much as honey," she replied, and the answer was sweet to his ears.

"And how much do you love me?" he asked the second.

"As much as sherbet," she replied, and the answer brought a sparkle to his eyes.

"And you?" he asked, turning to the third daughter.

"I love you as much as salt," she replied, and that answer was sour and bitter in his throat.

So the king made much of his two eldest daughters but drove the youngest away, out into the dark, lonely forest.

As she wandered sadly through the trees, she heard the clatter of a horse's hooves and hid in a hollow tree. But an edge of her dress fluttering in the breeze betrayed her, and the rider, who was a prince, called her out. As soon as he saw her, he loved her, and she him, and so they got married.

Meanwhile the king, her father, had grown weary of life with his two sweet-talking daughters. He decided to set out on a journey.

When he arrived at the prince's court, he was at once asked to feast there that night. His youngest daughter arranged for every dish to be a sweetmeat. The king took a taste of each one, but they did not satisfy his appetite; he began to despair of ever getting anything he could eat.

At last the daughter sent him a dish of spinach, such as poor farmers eat, seasoned with salt. The king ate it with relish.

Then the daughter threw back her veil and revealed herself. "Father," she said, "forgive me if it offends you, but I still love you as much as salt. My love may be simple, but it is true and lasting."

And the king saw what a fool he had been, embraced his daughter, and begged her forgiveness.

The Magic Lamp

MANY YEARS AGO there was a widow who lived with her only son in the capital city of a rich Rajah. One day she heard a knocking at her door.

"Hello, there!" A man stood outside the widow's house. From his clothes, she guessed he was a merchant.

"I've come to visit my younger brother," he said unexpectedly. "He lives here, doesn't he?"

The widow explained that her husband had died many years before, leaving considerable debts. Now she and her son were alone in the world, struggling to survive on what little they had. "But you're welcome to stay," she added.

The merchant agreed to do so, but after several days, bored with their frugal existence, he suggested that he and his nephew should try to change their fortune.

"Let's go and find the golden flowers," he said. "Pack us some food for our journey."

They set off at dawn and walked until the sun was high in the sky and the heat unbearable. Weary, the boy said, "I'm exhausted! I can't take another step." His uncle scolded him and set off again. On they walked, mile after long mile, until once more the boy said, "Uncle, please can we stop? My feet are killing me! I really can't go any further." His uncle was furious. Turning, he hit the boy with his walking stick. The boy was so terrified, he began to walk again, this time as fast as his uncle.

Eventually they came to a hill and climbed to the top to

collect firewood, but neither of them had anything with which to start the fire. "It doesn't matter," said the merchant, "just blow on the firewood as if you were kindling the flames."

The boy blew as hard as he could. He blew until he was red in the face. Finally he said, "Uncle, what is the use of blowing when there isn't a fire?"

The merchant replied, "Don't waste your breath! Blow or I will beat you."

The boy blew and blew until, gasping for breath, he said, "There isn't a fire. How do you expect it to burn?"

The merchant's only reply was to clout the boy on the head. Frightened, the boy blew even harder — and this time the firewood burst into flame.

When the fire died down, a trapdoor appeared underneath the ashes and the merchant told his nephew to pull it up. The boy grasped the handle and tugged. After some time, he said, "It won't budge!" The merchant told him to try harder. Afraid that he would be beaten if he didn't, the boy flexed his muscles and pulled with all his might, but eventually he had to admit defeat. "It's made of iron, it's much too heavy. I'm not strong enough to open it." The merchant was furious and hit him again, telling him to try harder.

This time the boy threw all his weight into lifting the trapdoor and, with a sigh, it opened. In the darkness beneath them, a lamp was burning and a huge pile of golden flowers glittered in the light it cast.

"Climb down and get those flowers," said the merchant, "but make sure you don't touch any of them until you've put out the lamp. Once you've done that, put as many flowers as you can on the golden tray and bring them back to me."

The boy did as he was told, but when be climbed back up to

the surface, he found he could not get out. "Please let me leave the flowers, Uncle. I can't get out," he said.

"No," said the merchant, "you must bring them to me."

"But I need to pull myself out, and I can't do that if my hands are full!"

At that, the merchant lost his temper and, slamming the trapdoor shut, abandoned the boy.

At first the boy waited patiently, expecting his uncle to return. He sat quite still, listening intently for the tiniest noise from above that would reassure him that he was not alone. Then he began to panic. He shouted until his voice was gruff from the strain. Finally, as the days dragged by, he wept with despair. Frightened and lonely sitting there in the dark, he picked up the lamp and started to polish it. When his signet ring rubbed against the lamp, a genie appeared. "What is your desire?" it asked.

"Please open the door and let me out," the boy replied. The next thing he knew, he was on his way home, taking the lamp with him.

When he finally reached home, the boy was starving, but there was nothing to eat in the house.

"This is quite a nice lamp," said the boy. "If I polish it up, I might be able to sell it and we could buy food with the proceeds." But as he rubbed it, his ring once again touched the lamp and the genie reappeared.

"What is your desire?" the genie asked.

"Rice, please!" said the boy.

Instantly huge bowls of sweet, steaming, cooked rice appeared and baskets of uncooked rice littered the floor.

A few days later, some horse traders passed the house. The boy decided he needed a horse. Once again he pressed his ring against the lamp and the genie appeared. When the boy asked for a horse, the genie instantly supplied him with a choice of hundreds.

Years went by and the boy grew up. He was down by the river one day when he saw the Rajah's daughter bathing. Unnoticed on the bank, he sat and watched her for some time. Then, returning home, he announced to his astonished mother, "I've seen the princess and I've fallen in love with her. Go to the palace and inform the Rajah that your son wishes to marry his daughter!"

His mother refused, saying that the Rajah would either think her mad or punish her for her impudence. But her son was insistent and finally she relented. She went to the palace and told the Rajah that her son wanted to marry the princess.

The Rajah, laughing, said he would agree to the marriage, but only if her son could produce a huge sum of money, greater than the Rajah's whole treasury.

Of course, the young man simply rubbed his lamp and he was able to give the Rajah three times what he had asked for.

But the Rajah had second thoughts. He was reluctant to see his daughter married to anyone other than a prince, so he demanded that a palace suiting her rank and station should be built before the marriage could take place.

The young man laughed and touched the lamp with his ring — the following morning a beautiful castle appeared on the edge of the city.

There was nothing for it. The Rajah had to admit defeat and the wedding took place.

A few years later, the Rajah and his son-in-law went hunting in the forests. While they were away, a merchant arrived at the castle. "Have you any old lamps that you want to get rid of?" he asked the princess. "I'll swap any old lamps you have for new ones."

The princess, thinking that it was about time she got rid of her husband's tarnished old lamp, gave it to him and received a new one in return. The wicked merchant, for it was none other than the young man's uncle, rubbed his ring on the lamp. The genie duly appeared.

"Take this castle and myself and the princess with it to my own country."

When the Rajah and his son-in-law returned, the castle had vanished without trace. The Rajah was reminded by his advisers that they had tried to dissuade him from the marriage — now look what had come of it! The Rajah, angry at the loss of his only daughter, sent for her husband and told him, "I will give you thirteen days to find her. If you do not find her by the end of the thirteenth day, on the morning of the fourteenth day you will die!"

The young man searched everywhere, but the thirteenth day arrived and the princess was still missing. Resigned to his death, he climbed to the top of a hill and lay down to sleep on a rock, exhausted. But when his ring struck the rock, another, lesser genie appeared.

"What do you want of me?" it asked.

"I have lost my wife and my palace," he replied. "If you know where they are, please take me to them!"

Instantly he was outside the gates of his palace, but it was in a strange land. There the genie left him.

Disguising himself, the young man went into the palace unobserved and found his wife. She told him that the merchant always wore the lamp on a chain around his neck so that no one could steal it.

"How can we get the lamp back?" asked the young man.

"Leave it to me," said the princess. "I'll drug his food. He's too greedy to notice!"

That evening, the merchant returned late and called to the princess to bring his supper. She brought him his food and, without even thanking her, he began to devour it noisily. He had eaten about half the meal when the drug took effect and he fell into a deep sleep. The young man tore the chain from the merchant's neck and rubbed the lamp with his ring.

Before dawn on the fourteenth day, the people of the city were amazed to find the palace back in its rightful place and the princess with it. The Rajah was so delighted to see his daughter again that he divided his kingdom in two and gave half to his son-in-law.

A Likely Story!

It was a warm day, the sky was clear and bright, and the hot air shimmered above the road. A moneylender was walking along a country lane, oblivious of his surroundings, thinking gloomily of money and how he could make the next few rupees. Rounding a corner, he saw a farmer ahead, and he quickened his step in order to catch up with him.

"Good morning!" said the moneylender.

"Morning," replied the farmer.

"I was just thinking how lonely I felt when I saw you. I shall enjoy the rest of my journey with someone to talk to. May I join you?"

"By all means," said the farmer, "but what shall we talk about? We haven't got much in common."

"I have an idea!" replied the moneylender. "We'll tell each other the tallest stories we can think of, and the first of us to doubt the other's story shall pay him one hundred rupees."

"What a great idea! Why don't you begin since you thought of it?" the farmer suggested, for he'd made up his mind that he would pretend to believe the moneylender's story no matter how wild it might be.

"Very well," replied the moneylender, "I will.

"I was walking along a road one day when I met a merchant leading a camel train laden with exotic goods."

"That's not unusual, I've seen one myself," murmured the farmer.

"The train stretched for a good half mile. A hundred and one camels, tied by their halters nose to tail. I counted them, so I know," continued the moneylender.

"So?" queried the farmer.

"Well, a kite swooped down and seized the leading camel in its talons. With ten great wing beats, the kite lifted it into the air and flew away with the camel and the hundred others that were tied to it."

"That kite must have been incredibly strong!" the farmer exclaimed.

"You doubt it?" asked the moneylender.

"No, not at all," responded the farmer, grinning. "Please carry on with your story."

"The princess of a nearby kingdom was sitting in her garden having her hair brushed by a maid. Her head was tipped back and she was gazing up at the sky, lost in thought, when the kite flew over. Just as it did, the lead camel kicked and the kite dropped its prey. All one hundred and one camels fell straight into the princess's left eye!"

"Ouch!" said the farmer, wincing. "I hate getting anything in my eye."

"Well, the princess leaped up and danced around, one hand over her eye, screaming, 'Oh! Oh! There's something in my eye and it HURTS!' "

"It would!" agreed the farmer. "So what did she do?"

"Her maid came running over to help. 'Keep still, your highness, and let me look!' Holding her head steady, the maid lifted the princess's eyelid. Out popped a camel, which she put into her pocket. Then she twisted up the corner of her head scarf, fished the other hundred out of the princess's eye, and popped them into her pocket too."

"Well, what happened next?" the farmer asked.

But the moneylender, who was quite breathless from story-telling, couldn't think of anything else to say. "That's the end. What do you think of that?" he asked.

"Wonderful," answered the farmer, "and so true to life."

"Well, it's your turn now," said the moneylender. "I'm longing to hear your story. I'm sure I'll find it interesting."

"Yes, I think you will," replied the farmer. "My father was a wealthy man. He had fifty cows, twelve oxen, half a dozen buffalo, and masses of goats. But his finest animal was a bay mare. He loved that horse more than anything."

"Yes, yes," interrupted the moneylender, "get on with it!"

"One day my father rode her to market in a new saddle. When he returned home, she had a saddle sore as big as the back of your hand!"

"So what?" said the moneylender impatiently.

"Well, it was June," continued the farmer, "the beginning of the rainy season, and there were dust storms in the air. The poor horse got dust and grains of wheat in the wound and, with all the wet weather, they began to sprout."

"Wheat tends to in wet weather and good soil," remarked the moneylender.

"The next thing we knew, there was enough wheat on that horse's back to fill our hundred-acre field. My father had to hire twenty men to harvest it!" said the farmer.

"What a good crop!" exclaimed the moneylender.

"Then your father, who had very little to his name," — the moneylender snorted — "came and, practically begging," — the moneylender glared but bit his tongue — "said to my father, 'I haven't eaten for over a week. Would you lend me half a ton of wheat? I'll be sure to repay you.'

"'Of course I will,' my father replied, 'take as much as you need and pay me when you can.'"

"Well?" demanded the moneylender, flushing with anger.

"Well, he took the wheat," the farmer answered, "but he never paid for it. It's a debt to this day. Sometimes I think I should talk to a lawyer about it."

The moneylender began counting on his fingers and mumbling under his breath.

"What on earth's the matter?" asked the farmer.

"The wheat is cheaper, I'll pay you for the wheat!" answered the moneylender, for otherwise he would have lost the contest and the hundred rupees.

To this day when a man owes a debt, the saying goes, "If you can't give me the money, give me the wheat."

The Boy Who Had a Moon on his Forehead and a Star on his Chin

MANY YEARS AGO, in a time when memory was young, there were seven daughters of poor parents, who were allowed to play together each day under the shady trees in the king's garden with their friend, the gardener's daughter. They often talked about their future lives, and the gardener's daughter always said: "When I grow up, I'm going to marry and have the most beautiful son in the world. He will be as beautiful as the sky at night, and he will have a moon on his forehead and a star on his chin." Everyone laughed at her, even her friends.

The only person who didn't laugh was the king, who had overheard her telling her friends one day. He was very taken with the idea. "I would like to have such a son," he said.

The king already had four wives, but none of them had had a son, let alone one with a moon on his forehead and a star on his chin. So he went to the gardener and told him that he wished to marry his daughter. The gardener and his wife were very flattered by this and wasted no time in inviting all their friends to the wedding.

Twelve weeks after their marriage, the gardener's daughter announced that she was expecting a baby. The king was overjoyed at this news, but his four other wives were insanely jealous. They kept their distance until the baby was almost due. Then they took to visiting the young girl each day, when the king was away, intent on making her life a misery. One day the four wives said to her, "My dear, we are concerned about you. The king is always out hunting. What happens if your baby arrives while he is out and we are not here to help you? What would you do on your own? You must find a way to get hold of him."

The girl fretted over this problem so much that when her husband returned, she asked him what to do if she fell ill or the baby was born while he was out.

"Don't worry, dearest," he replied, "I'll give you a kettle drum. No matter where I am or what I'm doing, I'll hurry back as soon as I hear you beating it."

Much relieved, the next day the girl told the four wives that the king had thought of a solution. She showed them the kettle drum and explained that she merely had to beat it and the king would come immediately.

"Why don't you try it out?" they asked slyly.

"Why should I call him from his hunting when I don't need him?" asked the girl.

"He won't mind being interrupted, and surely you want to be certain that he will come if you beat the drum," they replied. "Go on, give it a try!"

So at last, to please them, the girl beat the drum and summoned her husband.

"Why have you called me?" he asked. "You don't seem unwell."

"I only wanted to know if you would really come when I beat the drum. I'm sorry," she replied.

"Well, you can see that I will, so don't do it again unless you really need me!"

The next day, when the king had gone out again, the four wives came to see the gardener's daughter. They begged and begged her to drum once more.

"What if the king is miles away and cannot hear the drum?" they said. "Please set our minds at rest . . . and yours, of course. Go on, beat the drum!"

The gardener's daughter refused again and again until finally, worn out by their persistence, she beat the drum and the king came to her. He was furious when he discovered she was testing him again.

"That's the second time you've called me home needlessly!" he said. "From now on you can beat the drum as hard as you like but I shall not come!"

The following day the gardener's daughter felt the baby coming. Her husband was out, as usual, but no matter how hard or often she beat the drum, he assumed she was testing him once again and did not return.

The four wives told the frightened young girl that it was the local custom to bind a mother's eyes with a handkerchief during childbirth, and she would bring bad luck on her child if she did not.

"Quickly, bind my eyes!" the girl said tearfully.

Shortly afterward, she gave birth to a boy. He had two distinctive yet strangely beautiful birthmarks on his face. It was as if someone had trailed a finger in sepia ink and delicately etched a crescent moon on his forehead and a dimple, like a five-pointed star, in his chin.

The four wives whisked the child away before he made the slightest noise and handed him to a palace servant. "Either kill this child or hide him so well that his mother will never see or hear him," they said. "If you do this and do not breathe a word of it to anyone, we will give you one thousand rupees."

Then, returning to the girl's room, the wives put a large, round stone in the baby's crib. Taking the handkerchief from the young girl's eyes, they cried, "Look! Just look what you've produced! Look at your *son*!"

The poor girl was distraught. "What will the king say?" she kept repeating.

When the king returned and learned that his wife had given him a stone for a son, he flew into a terrible rage. Henceforth, he told her, she would be a palace servant. He would never speak to her again.

In the dark of night, the servant crept out of the palace, clutching a box with the prince inside. She carried it deep into the jungle until she found a huge clearing. There she dug a hole and, making sure the box was securely fastened, buried it with the boy still alive inside it.

She was so intent on her work that she didn't notice that the king's dog, Shankar, had followed her and was watching her every move. As soon as she had gone, Shankar dug up the box and opened it. When the dog saw the beautiful child, he vowed, "This child is more beautiful than a hunting hound and more vulnerable than the runt in a litter of puppies. I cannot eat anything so beautiful. I will protect him for as long as I live. I will swallow him whole and hide him in my stomach." And this the dog did.

Six months had passed when the dog decided to go back to the jungle to see how the boy had fared living in his stomach. And when Shankar let him out, the child was even more beautiful than before. But, unknown to the dog, his keeper had followed and seen everything.

Racing back to the palace, he met the four wives. "You won't believe what I've just seen!" he stammered with excitement.

"Shankar has a child living inside him — the most beautiful child you've ever seen. He has a moon on his forehead and a star on his chin!"

The four wives were terrified that they would be found out. Thinking fast, they tore their clothes, scratched their faces and arms, and made a terrible mess of their rooms. When the king returned, they rushed up to him. "Look at us! Your dog, Shankar, attacked us. We're afraid he might kill one of us next time!"

"I'm sorry he hurt you, my dears, but you're not to worry," reassured the king, "I'll have the dog shot tomorrow at dawn."

But Shankar overheard his master. He was determined that even if he had to die, the child would not, so he ran to the king's horse, Katar. Katar had a vile temper and was completely unmanageable, but he had always been courteous to Shankar.

"Katar, will you take great care of something very precious? The king intends to have me killed tomorrow, and there is no one else I can trust to take care of it."

"Show me what it is!" commanded Katar.

Shankar let out the child.

"What a beautiful child! I have never let anyone sit on my back, yet I would allow this child to ride me to the ends of the earth. You could not have chosen a better guardian for the boy, for I have magic in my blood. Rest assured, my friend, I will take great care of him. I am only sorry that *you* will not see him grow." And Katar swallowed the little prince.

"Thank you," Shankar said simply. "I will die happy tomorrow, knowing the boy is safe." And he did.

Katar let some time go by before he dared to see how the child fared. But the second time the horse risked playing with the prince, on the eve of the child's fifth birthday, a groom saw everything and rushed to tell the king's wives. Once again they tore their clothes, pulled out handfuls of hair, and scratched one another. By the time the king returned, they looked as if they had been dragged through a hedge backwards. They told the king that Katar had attacked them.

"Since no one can ride him, I have little use for him," said the king. "I'll have him shot in the morning."

The next day the king stationed an entire regiment of soldiers around the stables. "This horse is so wild, I don't think one bullet will be sufficient," he explained.

Katar, realising what was in store for him, let out the prince. As he was a magic horse, he also produced a saddle, a bridle, some exquisite clothes, a sword, and a gun.

"Put the saddle and bridle on me and the clothes on yourself. Buckle the sword 'round your waist and sling the gun over your shoulder!" Katar ordered. "Now climb up on my back!"

The boy did as he was told.

"Ready?" Katar asked. The boy nodded.

Katar burst out of the stables with the boy perched on his back. His appearance was so unexpected and his movement so fluid and fast that the soldiers didn't even have a chance to take aim before he was gone.

Katar galloped until nightfall, by which time he and the prince were in another country. That night they slept under a banyan tree, the boy curled against Katar's belly, his head on the horse's shoulder.

The following morning, when they woke, Katar told the prince the entire history of his birth and the strange circumstances of his early childhood. "When you are married, we shall

return. But now remove my saddle and bridle. Take off your clothes and tie them in a bundle with your sword and gun.'' Katar then produced some old threadbare clothes and told the prince to put them on.

''Now hide your bundle in the branches of this tree. You are a poor man now and must learn a trade. You should seek work with a merchant in the nearest city.''

''But I don't know anyone in this country. How will I find work?'' the boy replied.

''Don't worry, you'll find it soon enough. And if you ever need me, I'll be here,'' Katar said softly. ''Now you must go, but before you do, twist my right ear.''

The boy twisted Katar's ear and the horse turned into a donkey.

''Now twist your own right ear,'' Katar ordered.

The boy twisted his own ear and he became ugly. Only his beautiful eyes and voice remained the same.

Bidding farewell to Katar, the prince set off toward town and eventually found a grain merchant who needed a servant.

''I'm a poor boy looking for work,'' said the prince.

''Good,'' replied the grain merchant. ''I need a strong young lad to help me. You can be my servant.''

The merchant lived near the palace. One night, when he was fully grown, the prince was so hot that he wandered into the king's garden and lay by the marble pool. Drifting his fingers through the water, he began to sing a song of his homeland. The seventh and youngest daughter of the king woke up to the haunting notes and, dressing quickly, went out into the garden to see who it was who sang like a nightingale. She found a poor, ugly man with aquamarine eyes lying by the marble pool.

"Who are you and where do you come from?" she asked.

"I am the grain merchant's servant, your majesty," the prince answered. "I came from another country to seek service here and found work with him."

The princess nodded thoughtfully and returned to her room.

In the morning, she went to her father. "I want to marry, but I wish to choose my husband myself," she told him.

Since the king was very fond of his youngest daughter, he agreed to break with tradition and allow this. So he wrote to every king, rajah, and prince he knew of saying, "My youngest and most beloved daughter wishes to marry, but she insists on choosing her own husband. As I do not know who she wishes to marry, will you come to my palace on the tenth day of the tenth month so she can make her choice?"

On the tenth day of the tenth month it was as if the king's garden had been planted with people, for it was filled with noblemen from every corner of the known world. For each prince there were three servants looking curiously on. Among them was the ugly young man.

On the stroke of the tenth hour, the princess appeared in the east gateway on a richly decorated elephant. She was dressed in the rarest silks and she wore a simple gold chain around her neck. The elephant circled the garden three times, with the princess perched on top scrutinizing each face. On the fourth circuit, the elephant stopped by the west gate and the princess dismounted. Slipping past the rajahs and princes, she placed the necklace around the neck of the grain merchant's servant, to everyone's amusement.

"She's teasing us!" they cried. Tearing the necklace from the young man's neck and pushing him to one side, they shouted, "Out of the way, ragamuffin! Don't make our fine clothes dirty."

The princess toured the garden again, this time on foot. And once again she hung the necklace around the young man's neck. This time the suitors were furious. They tried to throw the young man out of the garden, but the princess forbade them to touch him. Gently placing him on the elephant's back, she took him to the palace.

Then the king stood up and said, "I promised my daughter that she could marry anyone she pleased. As she has twice chosen that poor, ugly man, she shall marry him. Thank you for coming. Please stay for the wedding celebrations if you wish."

So the princess and the young man were married the next day, and all the kings and rajahs and their sons returned home disappointed.

The princess's six sisters had all married rich, handsome princes, and they laughed at her for choosing such a poor, ugly man. Their husbands constantly taunted and humiliated him. Each day the six princes went hunting and returned laden with game for dinner. But the ugly young man remained in the palace at his wife's side.

"Why don't you ever go hunting?" the youngest princess asked one day. "You always stay here in the palace. Why?"

Her husband did not reply, but the next day he said, "I'm going out to taste the air."

"I'm glad you're going out for a change," said his wife. "Take one of the horses."

"No, I prefer to walk," her husband replied, and he set off immediately in order to reach the banyan tree early in the morning. Katar was waiting for him.

"Listen," the prince began, "I've married the youngest princess and everyone mocked her for choosing me, ugly and poor as I am."

"Twist my left ear!" snorted Katar.

The boy twisted Katar's left ear and he became a horse again.

"Now twist your left ear and you'll become yourself again," said Katar.

The boy twisted his left ear and there he stood, no longer a poor, ugly man but a handsome young prince with a moon on his forehead and a star on his chin. Climbing into the banyan tree, he found his bundle of clothes, his sword, and his gun, which seemed to have grown in size, just as he had done.

At dusk the prince mounted Katar and rode to the palace. As he rode through the city, people flocked from their houses to gape at the handsome young man with a moon on his forehead and a star on his chin. Arriving at the palace gates, he cried to the gatekeeper to let him in.

"I cannot, my lord, for I do not know you," replied the gatekeeper.

"I am the husband of the youngest princess. Now let me in!" commanded the prince.

"You jest my lord," laughed the gatekeeper. "The princess's husband is an ugly, common man like myself, and you are a beautiful prince."

"Nevertheless, I am he," said the prince. "Call the youngest princess here to me. I wish to speak to her."

When she came, the princess took one look at the handsome man and said, gracefully and simply, "My lord, I do not know why you wish to tease me in this way, but my husband does not look in the least like you. He is hunting at present and has not returned. Who are you, my lord? Why do you say you are my husband?"

"Because I *am* your husband."

"But most people will tell you that I married a poor, ugly man," said the princess, bewildered.

"That is true," agreed the prince, "but you yourself should know that appearances are deceptive. Beauty lies hidden in the most unexpected places. I was the grain merchant's servant when one night, when the heat was unbearable, I crept into your father's garden and lay by the marble pool, singing the song of my lost childhood. Hearing it, you came out to ask who I was and where I had come from. I told you that I had come from another country to look for work, and had found it with the grain merchant. You fell in love with my voice, I think . . . the hidden beauty that lay within . . . and you told your father that you wanted to marry, but that you yourself would choose your husband. Hundreds, no thousands, of suitors flocked to your father's garden on the tenth day of the tenth month, and in front of all of them, you chose me twice. Despite the laughter, the mockery and humiliation, you remained true to me and I to you. Look, I am still wearing the gold chain you placed around my neck and the ring you gave me on our wedding day. Do you still say I am not your husband?"

"Oh, my love, it is you! What a strange man you are! Why have you kept your beauty hidden all these years? Come, I must reintroduce you to my family."

Then, taking him by the hand, the youngest princess led him into the palace. Her parents were delighted that their best-loved daughter had chosen so well. Her sisters were secretly rather jealous that their sister was married to such a beautiful man, a man who seemed to have been touched by the moon and the milky way, with a crescent moon on his forehead and a star-shaped dimple on his chin.

Some weeks later, Katar told the prince that it was time to

return home. "Ask the king to let you return to your homeland so that you can introduce your wife to your father."

The prince always did exactly as Katar instructed, since he had good reason to trust him. So he said to his wife, "I long to return to my own home and see my father and mother, and I want them to meet you too."

"Very well," said the princess. "I will tell my father and mother and ask them to let us go."

The king, when consulted, said, "I am reluctant to let you go, but if you feel you must, I will send you in style!" He gave them elephants, camels, six hundred horses, and regiments of soldiers to guard them, as well as countless gifts for the prince's family.

Three days later, when the grand procession pitched camp outside the palace walls, the prince's father thought that someone had come to wage war on him. He was on the verge of calling a council of war when an envoy came from the prince bearing a letter which read: "You are a great king. Your fame has gone before you. I have come from afar to speak with you. Regard me as you would a son. As proof of my good intentions, I would like to invite all your people, old, young, rich, poor, whatever their estate, to a feast. Bring them to me here and I will feed them for a week."

The king was delighted and ordered all his people to go to the prince's camp for the grand feast the prince had promised them. Everyone went except the gardener's daughter. No one had told her to go, because no one had remembered that she existed.

When everyone was assembled, the prince saw that his mother was not there.

"Are you sure all your subjects are here?" he asked the king.

"Yes, quite sure," the king replied.

"Every single one?" the prince persisted.

"Every single one," affirmed the king.

"You're wrong!" said the prince. "The gardener's daughter, who was once your wife, is missing."

"You're right! I had forgotten her," exclaimed the king.

"Take my finest carriage and bring her here," said the prince, turning to his wife's handmaidens. "But first, bathe her in jasmine and dress her in the finest silk."

While they were waiting, the king studied the young prince. He could not help thinking ruefully that here was the son he had always wanted, the son that the gardener's daughter had promised him. A son more beautiful than his wild stallion, Katar. A son with the mark of the moon on his forehead and the mark of a star on his chin.

When the carriage arrived, the prince himself helped the gardener's daughter out of it. Bowing deeply, he brought her into the tent. The king's four wives were most put out. When they had arrived, he had not paid them the slightest attention.

At dinner the prince waited on the gardener's daughter himself. He offered her food from the best dishes and wine from his own cup.

"Who is this wonderful young man with a crescent moon on his forehead and a star on his chin?" she thought.

After two or three days of feasting had passed, the king could contain himself no longer. "Forgive me," he said, "but who are you and where do you come from?"

"Let me ask you a question," the prince replied. "Do you have any children?"

"No," said the king.

"Then you really don't know who I am?" asked the prince.

"No," said the king. "Please tell me."

"I am your son," said the prince. "The gardener's daughter is my mother. She always promised that she would give you a son with a moon on his forehead and a star on his chin, did she not?"

"Yes, yes!" said the king. "But how can you be my son and she your mother when I have never sired any children?"

"Ah, but you have!" said the prince. "Your four wicked wives told you that the gardener's daughter had given birth to a stone. They tricked both you and her. It was they who put the stone in my crib, and it was they who tried to kill me."

The king longed to believe him but could not. "I wish you were my son, but how can you be?"

"Do you remember Shankar, your dog, and how you had him killed? Who was it who encouraged you to kill him? It was your four wives, wasn't it? And now . . . " he said, pointing to his horse, " . . . don't you recognize this horse?"

"Why, yes," said the king, after a moment's hesitation, "that is my horse, Katar."

"Do you remember how you intended to kill him too, and how he rushed out of the stables with a small boy on his back when no one had been able to ride him?"

"Yes, yes!" cried the king. "Tell me everything!"

Then Katar himself told the king everything that had happened, from the moment of the prince's birth to the present time.

"This is wonderful, wonderful news! I have a son!" cried the king. "You must come and live with *me* now."

"That I cannot do," said the prince. "I only came to fetch my mother. Now that I have found her, I must return to my new home."

"But now that I've found you, I can't let you go," gasped the king. "You and your wife must come and live with me."

"We will never do that unless you banish your four wives for their wickedness."

"Consider it done," said the king and he turned to his four wives. "I do not know how you can live with this on your conscience. Leave this country at once and never return." Then he crossed to the gardener's daughter and, bowing reverently, told her, "I have wronged you terribly. How can you ever forgive me?"

The gardener's daughter, who looked as young and graceful as the day the king had married her, replied with simplicity, "My lord, what is there to forgive? We were both deceived by your other wives. You were wronged just as sorely as I was wronged. But now we both have a son. And such a son! He is the son we both wanted. A son with a moon on his forehead and a star on his chin."

"What a fool I have been," said the king and, looking at the gardener's daughter rather shyly, he added, "Would you come and live with me as my wife once again?"

"Of course," the gardener's daughter replied and, taking the hand that the king proffered, she allowed herself to be seated between her husband and her son.

The Brahman's Luck

Once there was a poor Brahman who knew all the holy scriptures and could read fate in the stars. But for all his learning and skill he could not earn a living. His wife would often scold him, saying, "You're not reading that astrological rubbish again, are you? How many times do I have to tell you that all the horoscopes, charts, and books in the world won't help feed and clothe us?"

The Brahman tried to ignore his wife but, as usual, it was a futile attempt. Closing his book with a sigh, he said, "And how many times have I got to tell you that God only gives when the time is right. There's no point in seeking employment now, because at present my ruling planet is Saturn and bad luck will follow wherever I go."

"What a load of nonsense! You just can't be bothered to get off your backside to do a decent day's work."

"Look, I can't say I blame you for being miserable when we are so short of money, but with such an unlucky horoscope, what do you expect me to do?"

"I expect you to call on the local Rajah for a start. He is pretty generous. I'm sure you could persuade him to part with some money if you tried."

"It's no use, I told you," the Brahman protested. "My stars tell me that I've got another six months of poverty and hardship ahead of me. The Rajah may think that I'm the greatest philosopher he's ever met, but I won't be any better off, I promise you."

"Oh, for heaven's sake! If you believe all that mumbo jumbo, you'll sit around doing nothing for another six months!" his wife exclaimed.

This was too much for the Brahman. He put down his book, saying grudgingly, "All right, all right, if you want me to go, I'll go. But don't say I didn't warn you."

So the Brahman set off. He was not young anymore, and it took him four days to reach the Rajah's palace. The Rajah was just going out to bathe and make an offering to the souls of his dead parents when the Brahman was announced. Treating the old man with the utmost respect, the Rajah himself found the Brahman a seat and asked, "To what do I owe this pleasure?"

The Brahman answered, "Your majesty, I have come to make a complaint. Thwarted by your power, poverty and distress have fled from this city with your generosity in hot pursuit. The two criminals, finding no other place to go, have taken refuge in my house and will not leave."

"I've never heard anything put so well in my life!" exclaimed the Rajah. "And believe me, I've heard it all in my time. You are a true philosopher, poet, and scholar. What on earth can I give to a man such as you?" Then, realizing he was still holding his two copper offertory pots, he thrust these into the Brahman's hands. "Take these! These are the bowls I use myself when praying for the souls of my parents. I can think of nothing more fitting to give to you."

The Brahman was thunderstruck, but he gave the Rajah his blessing and left. "Horibol Hori!" he said to himself, "What did I tell my wife? But would she listen? Oh, no! Eight days' walk and only two pots to show for it."

The Brahman finally got home a day later than expected. Before he even got through the door, his wife asked, "Well, what have you got?"

"'What have I got?'" he echoed. "More than any man could ask for!"

"Tell me! Tell me!" his wife squealed.

"A gift the Rajah has given to no other. The greatest gift he could bestow — these!" said the Brahman sarcastically, holding out the copper pots. It was too much. Even his wife was at a loss for words.

Several days passed in silence, but the Brahman's wife soon began to nag him again.

"I know your last attempt was a disaster, but you really must try again. You're sure to have better luck," she said.

"There you go again! Do I have to keep repeating myself? I will not succeed until my horoscope improves," said the Brahman tersely.

"Oh, just once more," said his wife. "There's that other Rajah who is famous for his generosity, particularly to needy Brahmans. Pay *him* a visit. Something good is bound to come of it, I just know it will."

"Don't say I didn't warn you," said the Brahman, "but I can't stand being nagged all the time, so I suppose I'll have to go."

The Brahman's wife washed his clothes again and off he went, this time carrying a leaf umbrella and a bamboo walking stick. After a ten day walk, he arrived at the palace, dirty and crumpled. The palace was huge. Stone lions stood at each side of the imposing gateway, which was guarded by ten sentries. No one could enter without their consent. When the Brahman tried to do so, they pushed him back. Old and unsteady, he fell heavily to the ground, but he got back to his feet and approached one of the sentries. "Please let me pass. I must see the Rajah."

"A scruffy old man like you? You must be joking," the soldier replied.

"I am a Brahman, and I'm dusty because I've come a long way," said the Brahman.

"Clear off!" the sentry snarled.

The Brahman was sitting on the ground wondering what to do next when the gatekeeper came out. Seeing the Brahman, he asked, "What's the matter?"

When the Brahman had told his story, the gatekeeper felt quite sorry for him. "The Rajah has given strict instructions not to be disturbed," he said, "but I'll see what I can do."

"Thank you," said the Brahman. "I'll wait here for you."

When the gatekeeper told the Rajah that a Brahman wished to see him, the Rajah replied, "Send him in at once, and make sure that my men show him every respect."

The gatekeeper returned to the gate and beckoned the Brahman to join him. As he was passing through the gate, the sentry pointed at his umbrella and walking stick. "You must leave that rubbish here." The Brahman, not wanting to be knocked over again, did as he was told.

As soon as the Brahman entered the room, the Rajah leaped up and led him to a seat. "You are welcome, Brahman. Tell me, what do you do?"

"I am a potter, your majesty," replied the Brahman.

"But that's impossible!" exclaimed the Rajah. "A Brahman would never be a potter. That's far too humble an occupation for one such as you."

"Your majesty," the Brahman continued, "my soul is like clay, softened by the tears of my hungry wife and children. With that moist clay, I shape countless hopes and dreams, but ill fortune always shatters them. Thus I am a Brahman and a potter."

The Rajah was overwhelmed by this allegory. "That was

beautiful! I've met many men over the years, but none had a poetic gift such as yours. I wouldn't insult your intelligence by giving you money, but I can think of nothing else that is worthy of you."

The Rajah sat back frowning, deep in thought. Suddenly a huge smile lit up his features. Leaping from his throne, he crushed the Brahman to his chest and kissed him on both cheeks. "I can think of nothing to give a scholar such as you, so I embrace you," he said.

The gift of a regal embrace quite took the Brahman's breath away, but he blessed the Rajah and left. When he reached the gateway, he found that his umbrella and stick had been stolen.

When the Brahman finally arrived home two weeks later, his wife rushed to meet him. "What did he give you? What did he give you?" she asked impatiently.

"Come inside and I'll show you," her husband replied.

As soon as they were inside the house, the Brahman grabbed her by the shoulders and pulled his wife to him, crushing her in a tight embrace.

"What on earth are you doing?" she cried. "Let me go!"

"What's wrong?" asked the Brahman. "I'm only giving you what I got."

"What in heaven do you mean?" his wife demanded.

"Just what I say," he replied. "Because I was so superior, the Rajah gave me something he had given no other Brahman. He gave me the greatest gift he could think of — he embraced me like a true friend. Didn't I tell you that my horoscope was hopeless at present?"

The Brahman's wife was speechless, but finally she had to agree that he seemed doomed to failure.

Eventually the six months passed.

"Right!" said the Brahman's wife. "The six months are up. Saturn has passed through your chart. You'd better go and see the Rajah again."

"You're quite right, my dear. I'll set off straight away."

"Listen, dear," his wife continued, "you've often told me that when your horoscope is positive, everything will turn out well, even if you do something wrong. So this time, don't bother to flatter the Rajah. Hurl abuse at him instead and see what you get in return."

"That's exactly what I was thinking," said the Brahman. "Only I intend to hit him too!"

Having calculated which day and hour would be most propitious, the Brahman set off for the Rajah's palace. The gatekeeper recognized him immediately. Remembering the Rajah's response on his previous visit, he ushered the Brahman in.

As soon as the Brahman was announced, the Rajah strode over to meet him, his arms outstretched in welcome. Without warning, the Brahman struck him on the chest with his stick and knocked him to the floor. "Guards, kill this traitor!" the courtiers shouted in unison. The guards came running, swords drawn.

At that moment, with a rumbling roar and a cloud of dust, the ceiling fell in on the very spot where the Rajah had been standing a minute before. The Rajah, immensely grateful for his narrow escape, ordered his guards to sheathe their swords.

"How can I thank you?" he asked the Brahman. "I owe you my life." He turned to his courtiers. "Don't you see that the Brahman saved my life? If he hadn't pushed me out of the way, I would have been crushed. Had he just called out to warn me, I wouldn't have moved out of the way in time. I shall be in his debt for as long as I live. You must welcome him to the court, for I intend to keep him here, if he will stay."

The Brahman was only too happy to stay, particularly when the Rajah offered to build him his own mansion and provide him with anything he desired.

When she saw her husband two days later the Brahman's wife was speechless. He returned on an elephant, accompanied by the Rajah himself. She didn't ask him whether the planets had brought him good fortune. She didn't really have to.

The Thirsty Fool

THERE WAS ONCE A FOOL who forgot to take any water with him on his travels. He had been walking through a wood for several days and he was tormented with thirst.

At last he reached a river. But he did not drink. He just stood there, gazing in dismay at the flowing waters.

Someone saw him there and asked, "Why aren't you drinking? You look so thirsty."

The fool replied, "I *am* thirsty. But how could I drink all this?"

And with that the fool walked on, thirstier than ever.

Even the biggest river can only be drunk one gulp at a time.

The Wonderful Ring

MANY YEARS AGO there was a king who had two sons. When the king died, he did not leave his possessions to his eldest son as was usual, but shared them between the two princes. The younger son was a wastrel. He began to squander his inheritance so extravagantly that within a matter of months there was nothing left. Destitute, he asked his mother if she had any jewels left that he could sell.

"You've sold everything except my ring, but you may as well have that too," she replied tearfully.

So he sold the ring for four rupees and set off to make his fortune.

Half a mile along the road he met a man with a cat.

"How much do you want for your cat?" asked the prodigal prince.

"One rupee," the man replied.

"It's yours!" cried the spendthrift prince, and he gave the man one rupee.

By and by he met a man leading a dog and couldn't resist asking, "How much do you want for your dog?"

"One rupee," the man answered.

"Done!" said the prince, and he paid for it without another thought.

Next he met a man with a parrot.

"Will you sell your parrot?" the prince asked, and when he heard that the man would sell it for one rupee, he promptly bought it.

He had just one rupee left, but when he met a snake charmer carrying a cobra, he asked without hesitation, "How much is it?"

"Only one rupee," the man replied.

"What a bargain," said the prince, handing over the last of his money.

So now the prince had a cat, a dog, a parrot, and a snake, but his pockets were empty. Realizing that he couldn't afford to feed them properly, he set to work to earn some money. But he wasn't used to hard work, and by the end of each day, he was exhausted.

The snake, feeling sorry for the kind young man, said, "If you are not afraid to come and see my father, he might reward you for saving me from the snake charmer."

The young prince wasn't afraid of anything, so he agreed to go. When they arrived at the cobra's house, the serpent told the prince to wait outside while he prepared his father for the prince's visit. When the snake's father heard that the prince had rescued his son, he promised to give him anything he desired.

As the young cobra showed the prince into his house, he whispered in his ear, "My father says he will give you anything you want for saving my life, but take my advice and only ask for his little ring as a memento."

The prince was somewhat surprised — a ring wasn't much use to him — but he trusted the snake, so he did as he was told. When the snake's father asked what he desired for rescuing his son, the prince replied, "Thank you, but I have everything I need." When the snake's father asked a second time, the prince replied that he had all he could wish for. But when the snake's father asked for a third time what he could give to the man who

had saved his son's life, the prince answered, "Since you wish me to take something, can I have your ring as a keepsake?"

"You have dared to ask for my greatest treasure!" the snake hissed. "If I had not promised to give you anything you desired, I would turn you into ashes for your presumption. But since I have promised, it is yours. Take it and go!"

Taking the ring, the prince returned home with the young cobra.

"I shouldn't have listened to you!" he exclaimed. "I only made your father angry, and all I got was a worthless ring. I should have asked for money."

"You don't know how lucky you are," replied the cobra. "This ring is magic. Just ask, and it will give you whatever your heart desires."

The prince was delighted and thought he would put the ring to the test. "Ring," he said, "I am hungry. Please give me something to eat."

Seconds later, a delicious meal appeared. The prince consumed it with relish. Then, feeling well nourished for the first time in weeks, he set off lightheartedly for the city he had spotted on the skyline.

A soldier was nailing a proclamation to the city gates: "Whosoever can build a golden palace with golden stairs in the middle of the sea in the space of one night shall be given half this kingdom and the hand of the King's daughter in marriage. Whosoever tries and fails shall forfeit his life."

Still dusty and road-worn, the prince presented himself to the king, declaring himself a prospective suitor. The king showed him a list of those who had failed and tried hard to discourage him, but the spendthrift prince was adamant. "I am not afraid of anything," he said. "Besides, I know I'll succeed."

The king, irritated by the young man's boast, raised an eyebrow. "Very well, you may build your castle tonight, but I will post a guard to make sure you do not run away when you fail."

That evening the prince found a peaceful spot in the shelter of the cliffs and went to sleep. The guard shook his head. "Why waste your life for a stupid gesture?" he thought.

As the first fingers of light crept over the horizon, the prince said, "Oh ring, please build me a palace of gold with golden stairs in the middle of the sea."

Instantly the water began to curdle, and with a sound like thunder, a golden palace towered out of the sea, glowing softly in the early morning light. The guard ran to tell the king.

The king took one look at the miraculous palace and, as promised, offered his only daughter and half his kingdom to the spend-thrift prince.

"I don't need your kingdom and I don't want your daughter," said the prince. "I'll just keep the palace I built in the sea." But as soon as he set eyes on the princess, the young man changed his mind and married her.

Each day the prince went out hunting with his dog, leaving his wife alone in the palace with only the cat, the snake, and the parrot for company. On his return one evening, he found his wife crying bitterly. He asked her what was troubling her.

"I will never be as beautiful as this wonderful palace, but I long to be. Dear husband, will you turn me into gold?" she replied.

To please his wife, whom he loved dearly, the prince said, "Oh ring, turn my wife into gold." When he turned back to her, she was gold from head to foot.

One day when the princess was combing her hair, two golden strands came out in the comb. Thinking it would be such a waste to throw them away, she made a small boat from palm leaves and, laying the hairs inside it, set it afloat.

The boat was blown across the four seas to a distant kingdom, where a fisherman mending his nets was blinded by a strange dazzle in the shallows and waded into the surf to find out what caused it. Thinking he might receive a reward for the strands of gold, he took them to his king, who in turn showed them to his son. The prince took one look at the beautiful hair and vowed that he would not eat or drink until he had married the woman who possessed it.

The king, fearful that his son would die, called on the wisest woman in his kingdom and asked for her help.

"I will find the golden-haired princess," she said, "but you must give me whatever I desire in return."

"You will have whatever you desire," the king agreed.

"Then you must build me a golden barge with a silken seat," she declared.

When the boat was ready, the woman trained four enormous men to row tirelessly as she directed. If she raised her hand they shipped their oars, if she lowered it they bent their backs and stroked the boat smoothly through the water.

After many days on the ocean, they saw the golden palace. The woman raised her hand, the oarsmen stopped rowing, and the barge slowly glided toward the landing. The woman stepped out and climbed the steps into the palace. She quickly found the golden princess. Taking her by both hands, she kissed her on each cheek, saying, "Don't you recognise me, dear? I'm your aunt."

The princess didn't believe the woman at first because she

didn't look at all familiar, but the woman soon convinced her that they were related. Glad to have company, the princess invited the woman to stay for a few days and was soon chatting to her as if she'd known her for years.

"How can you live alone in this palace without any servants?" the old woman asked.

"My husband has a magic ring which he wears night and day," the princess replied. "He wishes on the ring and we get whatever he has asked for."

"But what would become of you if anything happened to the prince?" the woman asked. "Surely it would be wiser for you to keep the ring."

The princess had never considered this prospect before, but now her imagination ran riot. On her husband's return that evening, she said to him, "My darling, if anything were to happen to you, what would become of me? I am all alone in this palace and I would not survive without you or that ring of yours. Would you let me look after it during the day?"

"You mustn't worry yourself, my darling, but if it will reassure you, then of course you must have it," replied the prince, and the next morning he left the ring in her safekeeping.

As soon as the prince was gone and she was sure that the princess had the ring, the woman persuaded her to go and look at the golden boat which was moored at the foot of the stairs. It took only a little more encouragement to coax the princess into the boat for a short trip along the coastline. Once she was aboard, the woman signed to the oarsmen to row.

The princess soon begged to be taken back home, but the woman ignored her and the oarsmen rowed on. After several days, the golden boat docked with its captive and the woman announced that she had found the prince's golden bride and they could marry at once. However, the princess had other ideas.

"I am already married," she said. "If my husband does not come for me within six months, I will consider remarrying, but not before then."

The prince was happy to wait for six months. It was unlikely that the princess's husband would find her — and even if he did, the prince would arrange a warm welcome and a cold end for him.

The spendthrift prince was beside himself. He had returned to his parrot, cat, and snake, but there was no sign of his wife.

"She's gone off with her aunt in a golden boat," the parrot told him. "But don't despair! The cat and I will find her."

The parrot and the cat journeyed from house to house, from city to city, from land to land until at last they found the golden princess. Fluttering down beside her, the parrot asked, "Where is the magic ring?"

"My so-called aunt keeps it under her tongue," the princess said, "so no one can take it from her."

The parrot consulted the cat. "My dear fellow, nothing could be easier," said the cat. "The princess must ask for rice for supper tonight, but she must save some. When the old woman is asleep, she must scatter the rice in front of the rat hole in their room. Then leave the rest to me."

That night the princess picked at her food and left most of the rice on her plate. When the woman fell asleep, the princess got up and sprinkled the rice in front of the rat hole.

It was past midnight and the room was quiet when the rats emerged to eat the rice, but the cat was waiting for them. Pouncing on the rat with the longest tail, the cat dragged it to

the old woman, who lay on her back with her mouth wide open, snoring. The cat forced the rat's tail up the woman's nose. When she woke with a tremendous sneeze, the ring shot out of her mouth and onto the floor. In a flash of scarlet and blue, the parrot seized the ring in its beak and flew out the window.

The prince was sitting on the landing, his feet in the water, when the magic ring dropped into his lap. He looked up. The parrot was hovering above him. "Stop daydreaming!" it squawked. "It's taken me three days to reach you and there isn't a moment to lose! You must get the princess back."

The prince closed his eyes. "Ring," he said fervently, "please bring my wife back to me!"

When he opened his eyes, there she was, a golden princess for his golden castle.

Three Fussy Men

VISHUSVAMIN WAS PREPARING to make a sacrifice when he realized he was missing one vital ingredient. ''Go and get me a turtle,'' he told his three sons.

The three brothers wandered up and down the beach until they found a turtle basking in the sun. The eldest took one look at it and said, ''I'm not touching that — it's covered with slime. One of you two will have to take it to Father.''

His brothers immediately bridled. ''Why should we take it if you won't?''

''Because our father won't be able to make his sacrifice properly if you don't,'' the eldest son replied.

''So what?'' said the younger brothers. ''That still doesn't explain why *we* have to take it rather than you.''

''Don't be stupid!'' exclaimed the eldest brother. ''You know perfectly well that I'm most particular about food of any kind. Being so fussy, I can't be expected to touch that revolting thing.''

''You may be fussy about food,'' said the middle brother, ''but I'm the real connoisseur. To see a woman of less than flawless beauty makes me break out in hives, so I don't see why I should take it either.''

''Huh! Don't look at *me*,'' said the youngest. ''If you expect me to take it, you can think again. I'm the fussiest of us all. Just think how particular I am about where I sleep.''

The three brothers began to argue so heatedly that they forgot all about the turtle. They decided that only the king could judge which of them was the most particular.

The king listened carefully to the three brothers. Then he said, "I will test each of you. We will find out who is the most discerning."

The king clapped his hands and demanded a meal to be brought in. Servants entered carrying huge platters of steaming rice and curry and bowls piled high with pineapple and mango. Everyone began to eat — except the eldest brother, who retched and held his nose.

"Why don't you eat anything?" asked the king. "It's delicious!"

"This rice stinks like the ashes from a funeral pyre," the eldest brother replied. "I can't bring myself to eat it."

The king ordered everyone else to smell the food. The response was unanimous: "This rice smells sweet and fragrant and is quite delicious."

But still the eldest brother refused to eat it.

The king was intrigued. He sent word to the cook, demanding to know where the rice had come from. To his amazement, he learned that the rice had been grown in a field near a burning ghât, where bodies are cremated.

"Your taste buds are very subtle," said the king to the eldest brother. "Eat what you like from any other dish."

After dinner the king beckoned to the most beautiful woman in the palace. "Go and entertain my guests," he commanded.

The three men watched her approach. The eldest brother was completely smitten, and the youngest was tongue-tied, but the middle brother turned his head away in disgust. "Ugh!" he said. "She smells like a goat!"

"How can you say such a thing?" the king exclaimed. "This lady bathes in sandalwood and jasmine oil. You must apologize at once."

But the middle brother refused. The king, exasperated by his

rudeness, questioned the lady, only to discover that she had been reared on goat's milk as a child. "I am most impressed," he said. "You are as discerning as your brother."

On retiring for the night, the youngest brother took one look at his bed and asked for six more mattresses in order to be comfortable. His bed was duly made up with seven mattresses and fine silk sheets and the young man lay down to sleep. But just before midnight, he woke up screaming and doubled up in agony. There was a red mark on his side as if something had pressed deeply into his skin. When the king was told, he ordered his servants to check under the mattresses. One by one the mattresses were removed. Under the last was a single human hair.

When the king saw the hair and the scar it had left on the youngest brother's body, he was astonished. "How can your skin be so sensitive through seven mattresses?" he asked.

The following day the king called the brothers together. "I cannot say which of you is the most refined," he told them, "so I shall give each of you three hundred thousand gold pieces. You may stay at my court for as long as you wish, for I need men of discernment around me."

The three brothers were only too happy to oblige. Flattered by the king's praise and seduced by his generosity, the brothers forgot their father's request. Oblivious to the fact that they had sinned by obstructing their father's sacrifice, they remained in the palace for the rest of their lives.

The Mouse–Girl

ONCE UPON A TIME a holy hermit found a young mouse that had escaped from the claws of a bird of prey. He took pity on the creature and adopted it. He was so holy that by the sheer force of prayer he managed to turn the mouse into a girl.

The hermit brought the child up in his hermitage, and when she was grown, he began to cast around for a suitable husband for her. His first choice was the sun. "Marry this girl, for I wish her to marry a powerful husband," he said.

But the sun replied, "The cloud is more powerful than I, for he can obscure me in a moment."

So the holy man called the cloud. "Marry this girl."

But the cloud said, "The wind is more powerful than I, for he can blow me wherever he pleases."

So the holy man called the wind. "Marry this girl."

But the wind said, "The mountain is stronger than I, for I cannot move him."

So the holy man asked the mountain, "Will you marry this girl?"

But the mountain replied, "The forest mouse is stronger than I, because he can dig holes in me."

So the holy man called the forest mouse to him and said, "Marry this girl."

"Gladly," replied the mouse. "But how will she get into my hole?"

"I see," said the holy man, "that we must end as we begin. It is better that she should be a mouse again." So by his prayers he turned her back into a mouse, and she and the forest mouse were married.

The Brahman, the Tiger, and the Six Judges

A TIGER HAD BEEN TERRORIZING the countryside and had killed countless animals before the villagers managed to capture and cage it. One day a Brahman happened to pass the cage and the tiger cried out to him, "Stranger, help me. I am dying of thirst. Please let me out so I can drink."

"I wouldn't dream of it. I'm not stupid! You'll eat me if I release you," the Brahman replied.

"What if I promise not to? Please, I implore you, just open the cage so I can drink some water and then I'll jump straight back in again," the tiger begged.

At this, the Brahman took pity on the tiger and opened the cage. No sooner had he done so than the tiger leaped out, snarling, "I think I'll eat you first and have a drink later!"

"Just a minute!" said the Brahman. "You can't kill me without a trial. We will find six judges, and they will decide whether I deserve to live or die."

"That seems fair enough," said the tiger.

So the Brahman and the tiger walked on together until they came to a huge banyan tree. "Will you pass judgment on what I have to tell you?" the Brahman asked the tree. The tree replied that it would.

"Well," said the Brahman, "I let this tiger out of his cage to drink some water, but now that I have freed him, he threatens to eat me. Is that fair?"

The tree replied, "Men like to sit in the shade of my branches to avoid the midday sun, but they often break my branches and tear off my leaves for no good reason. I think the tiger should eat the man because men are never grateful."

The tiger was about to pounce on the Brahman when the man pointed out that they still had five other judges to consult. "Very well," said the tiger. "Let us find another judge."

So they wandered on until they came across a camel.

"Camel, will you judge my case?"

"What shall I judge?" the camel asked.

When the Brahman had explained how the tiger had tricked him and now intended to eat him, the camel replied, "When I was young and strong and able to work hard, my master took good care of me and gave me plenty of good food. Now that I am old and decrepit, he starves me and beats me all the time. Let the tiger eat the man, for men are ungrateful wretches."

The tiger would have killed the Brahman there and then, but the Brahman said, "Not so fast! We have only heard two judges."

A little further on they met a bullock lying by the roadside.

"Will you judge our case?" asked the Brahman.

"Tell me what I must judge," said the bullock.

"I found this tiger in a cage," said the Brahman. "He begged me to free him so that he could drink some water, but as soon as I did, he threatened to eat me. Is this fair?"

"When I was able to pull a heavy load, my master looked after me and fed me well. Now that I can no longer work, he has left me here by the roadside to die. The tiger should eat the man, for men have no compassion."

The Brahman still did not lose hope, even though three judges had recommended that the tiger should eat him. He was determined that they should ask the other three judges.

Just then an eagle swooped low over their heads and the Brahman cried out, "Eagle, will you pass judgment on our story?"

"Tell me your story," the eagle replied.

So the Brahman told his story again, embellishing it a little. When he had finished, the eagle responded, "Men shoot me for sport. They climb up to my nest and steal my eggs. The tiger is welcome to eat the man, for men are tyrants and bullies."

The tiger roared, "Everyone is against you Brahman. I am going to eat you!"

But the Brahman replied, "Not yet. We have two more judges to question."

A short while later they found a crocodile, and once again the Brahman asked him to judge his case, hoping for a better response. But the crocodile said, "Whenever I put my nose above the water, some man tries to kill me. As long as there are men around, I shall have no peace. The tiger should eat you."

The Brahman was as good as dead, but he persuaded the tiger to let him find his sixth judge. "If you must," said the tiger wearily.

Eventually they met a jackal. The Brahman related his story again, then asked in trepidation what his judgment might be.

"I cannot pass judgment on this case," the jackal replied, "unless I know exactly where each of you was at the time. Show me." So they all returned to the cage.

"Now, Brahman," said the jackal, "show me where you were standing."

The Brahman went and stood by the cage.

"Right there?" asked the jackal.

"Yes," replied the Brahman.

"Now where were you?" he asked the tiger.

"In the cage, of course," said the tiger.

"Yes, but which way were you looking?" asked the jackal.

"I'll show you," said the tiger, jumping into the cage.

"Fine," said the jackal. "But was the door open or shut? I need to have all the facts."

"It was locked," said the Brahman.

"Then shut and bolt it," said the jackal.

When the Brahman had done this, the jackal said, "You are a wicked, ungrateful tiger. The Brahman freed you out of the goodness of his heart and you wish to repay his kindness by eating him? Stay there and rot for the rest of your days!"

And the Brahman and the jackal went on their separate ways.

The Prince Who Was Changed into a Ram

THERE WAS ONCE A KING with sixteen hundred wives, but only one child, a son. The king's single ambition for this son was to find a wife for him.

"She won't be just any princess! She'll be as delicate but as strong as a spider's web, and she'll be the only daughter of a rich and powerful king who has as many wives as I have."

But such a girl proved hard to find. None of the king's councillors could manage it. Finally the king consulted his wisest advisor, a talking parrot of extraordinary intelligence. The parrot agreed to fly as far afield as necessary, around the world if he had to, in order to find the right princess. He set off immediately, a portrait of the prince strapped to one of his legs so that he could show it to the princess when he found her.

Crossing the border just before dawn, the parrot flew straight into an electric storm. Buffeted and blown, wet and weary, he saw a hollow tree and decided to shelter in it until his feathers dried. But as he was about to fly into the hollow trunk, a voice said, "Do not enter or you will be blinded!" Wisely, the parrot perched on a twig and awaited developments. A few minutes later, a mynah bird flew out of the hollow trunk, perched next to the parrot, and said, "I had to say that or you'd have flown in on top of me and I needed a quiet breather. I'm exhausted! I've been flying nonstop for weeks, trying to find the impossible!"

"What are you looking for?" asked the parrot, his curiosity piqued.

"A prince for our princess. But he can't be just any old prince — he must be the only son of a rich and powerful king with sixteen hundred wives. And the princess says he must be good looking."

"Have a look at this," said the parrot, and he showed the mynah the prince's portrait. "My prince is just the man you're looking for. The only question is, is your princess as beautiful?"

"She certainly is. What luck!" cried the mynah. "Fly back with me and show your portrait to the princess and her father, and we'll see what they have to say."

When the parrot and the mynah flew into the throne room, the mynah perched on the king's right knee and the parrot on his left.

"You will not believe what has happened," the mynah began. "Fate decreed that I should meet this parrot, for it turns out that we both belong to a wealthy, brave, and wise king with sixteen hundred wives. One king has an only son, one an only daughter. The parrot is searching for a wife for his prince; I am searching for a husband for your daughter." Then, turning to the parrot, he said, "Show him the portrait."

The king was delighted by this story and by the portrait, which he sent to the women's quarters to ask the opinion of his wives. Hours passed, then days, while all sixteen hundred wives studied the portrait. At last it was the princess's turn. She immediately fell in love with the man in the portrait and would not let it out of her sight. So the wives sent word to the king, and the king ordered the parrot to return to his master with the good news. "Ask him to prepare the prince for marriage, and send him to me in four months' time."

When the parrot returned home, the prince's father began to make elaborate arrangements for his son's wedding: six

hundred horses with the finest buffalo skin saddles, ten thousand foot soldiers in special uniforms, the finest silk robes and saris for the prince and his future wife, the rarest fruit and spices for the princess's father, the most delicate perfumes for his sixteen hundred wives, and the most exquisite jewels for everyone. But three days before the appointed wedding day, the prince's father suddenly fell ill and died. The prince had to delay his departure in order to give his father a state funeral and observe the proper weeks of mourning.

When he finally set off with the parrot leading the way, it took him two days to reach the princess's kingdom. That night he camped in the garden below the palace wall, within sight of the princess's rooms, in order to be near her.

Then everything started to go wrong. First a gardener shot the parrot for stealing dates. Then the king was angry because the prince was late. In vain the young prince tried to explain about his father's illness. The king simply would not listen.

But the king had reckoned without his daughter. The princess had seen the prince wandering around the garden below her window and was more in love than ever. That night she ate only half her meal. Handing the rest to her servant, she said, "Take this to the prince. Tell him it is the princess's own food, which she wishes him to have. If he refuses to eat it, tell him to look inside the nan bread."

The prince, while flattered that the princess wished to share her food with him, was afraid that it might have been tampered with, so he refused to eat it. But inside the nan bread he found his portrait.

"It's my portrait!" he said aloud. "She's trying to tell me something. Could it be that she loves me still?"

He motioned to the servant to stay for a moment, then sat down and wrote the princess a love letter.

At midnight the prince woke to a gentle touch on his cheek. "Don't be surprised," said the princess softly. "I already knew that my destiny lay with yours, and your letter confirmed it. But my father will never consent to our marriage, so we will have to flee to your country. Saddle your horse. We must set off right away."

The night was dark with only a sliver of moon to light the way, but they galloped recklessly along the dusty road, stopping briefly to rest for a few hours before daybreak. After another full day on the road, they spent the night in a small hill village. But unfortunately, there was only one place to stay, and that was with the village witch.

The witch had an only daughter, who fell in love with the prince at first sight. She was determined to have him to herself. The witch had always given her daughter anything she desired, so while the princess was distracted and the prince was inspecting the rooms, she threw a cord around the prince's neck, muttered an incantation, and changed the prince into a ram. From that moment, the prince was bound to the witch's daughter by the cord around his neck. By day, with the cord in place, the ram followed her like a shadow. By night, the ram became a prince again, but he had forgotten all about the princess.

The princess, in the meantime, was upset and confused. One minute the prince was with her, the next he had vanished. She did not know whether he had been killed or deserted her, but she was determined to find out. Disguising herself as a man, she presented herself at court. Impressed by her intelligence and wit, the king was persuaded to appoint her a deputy police inspector.

Many secrets of many houses were known to deputy inspectors, and the new deputy inspector used every means at her disposal to find the prince — but he could not be found. In the course of her inquiries, however, she learned that the woman in whose house she and the prince had stayed was a witch, and her intuition told her to keep an eye on the household.

She returned to the house often, but though the ram was always there, she had no idea that it was her beloved. Gradually a friendship sprang up between her and the witch's daughter. Like everyone else, the witch's daughter was blissfully unaware that the deputy inspector was a woman, and she slowly fell in love with her. She began to give the deputy inspector gifts, tokens of her affection, each one more exotic than the last.

One of these presents was a bolt of cloth, which the deputy inspector hung in her window. The cloth was so cleverly woven that when the light and the wind caught the material, the jewel-like animals in the design seemed to stir and glow, pulsing with a life of their own.

It wasn't long before the queen heard of the miraculous material and asked if she could have some for her rooms. The deputy inspector immediately sent every scrap of material she had, but on seeing it the queen decided that every room in the palace should have some. She begged the deputy inspector to find her some more.

"I think that might prove difficult," said the deputy inspector, "but I'll try." And she hurried to the witch's house to ask where she could find more cloth.

"Where is not a problem. It's how you'll get it that worries me," said the witch. "The cloth was sent to me by my brother, who lives on an island on the other side of the great ocean."

"Well, write and ask him to send you some more," said the deputy inspector.

"I can't," said the witch. "My brother is a wizard. He has killed everyone else on the island so that he can keep its riches for himself. Now he is the only living creature there except for a pack of lions, which he keeps as watchdogs. He feeds them only pampas grass, which they hate. Consequently they kill anyone who sets foot on the island. How can I send a messenger, knowing that he will lose his life?"

"Then I'll have to go myself," said the deputy inspector. "If I don't, the queen will make my life such a misery, it won't be worth living. So tell me where to find your brother's island, and I will go to see him."

"Wait!" said the witch. "My daughter loves you, so I must help you — even if it is against my own brother." She produced a small clay jar which hung on a thong around her neck. "This jar contains my brother's soul. If I smash it, he will die, the lions will be free to eat what they choose, and you will be safe." The witch dashed the jar to the ground. "Now go, and good luck go with you."

The following day the deputy inspector left on an expedition to obtain more material. On crossing the great ocean, she quickly found the island and the wizard's house, which was piled with cloth and jewels, each more beautiful than the last. Laden with treasure, she returned to the king, who was so pleased with his deputy inspector that he made her his heir.

A few years passed, the old king died, and the deputy inspector succeeded him. Now that she was king, she was more determined than ever to find her lost love. Suspecting that the witch had caused the prince's disappearance and that her daughter's ram had something to do with it, she ordered every ram in the city to be brought to her. She examined the rams personally, speaking to them, stroking them, looking deep into their eyes, but none seemed to recognize her.

Puzzled, she asked her police inspectors to make sure no rams had been hidden. When they arrived at the witch's house, they found her daughter feeding the ram. She tried hard to hold on to the charmed cord, but the policemen tugged it away from her and led the ram to the king, with the witch and her daughter in tow. As they approached, the ram ran toward the king, the cord broke, and there stood the prince, still young and beautiful.

"I have not forgotten that you helped me win this crown," the king told the witch, "but I cannot condone your wickedness in bewitching this prince. You and your daughter are banished to the island where your brother once lived." Then she turned to the prince. "My lord, stay in my palace tonight. I have much I wish to tell you."

Later that night, the king revealed her true identity to the prince and told him how she had come to be king. Delighted to be reunited, they decided to face the people together the following morning and tell them the truth about their king.

At noon on the following day, the whole city gathered at the palace walls to hear what the king had to say. Standing beside her prince, the princess spoke: "Look on me! I am your king and yet I am a woman. I have the courage of a man, yet I am a woman. To find the prince, my husband, I disguised myself as a man, yet I used a woman's wits. Now we wish to rule together, as king and queen. Will you have us?"

And the people drowned any further words with their wild cheers.

The Boy and his Stepmother

ONCE THERE WAS A BOY who spent every day tending a cow while it grazed. The boy was getting thinner each day — anyone could see that. The cow began to get worried.

"What's wrong with you?" she asked. "You've looked after me since you could barely reach my knee, and you weren't so skinny then. Aren't you eating properly?"

"My stepmother starves me," the boy replied.

"Well, don't tell anyone and I'll give you some food," said the cow. "Go and get some banana leaves and weave yourself a plate from them."

The boy fetched the leaves and fashioned a crude bowl. The cow leaned over the bowl and shook her left horn. Rice poured out of it in a creamy torrent. Then turning her head to shake the other horn, the cow poured relish over the rice.

The boy quickly grew stronger and fatter on this rich diet, and his stepmother, suspecting that he was stealing food from her, watched him closely. She followed him everywhere, and eventually she saw the cow feeding the boy.

"Hah! I'll teach them! Think they can cheat me out of food, do they? Well, we'll see," she said to herself.

Feigning illness, she told her servants that the cow had jinxed her and she would die unless it was killed. Her servants agreed to do it on the following day. But the boy overheard and ran to tell the cow.

"Listen very carefully," said the cow. "Make a rope of rice straw. It doesn't have to be perfect — some bits can be fat, others thin. Put it somewhere obvious so that the servants will find it and tie me up with it. Just as they are about to kill me, grab hold of my tail and pull as hard as you can."

The next afternoon the servants found the rope and used it to tie the cow to a stake. The boy quickly grabbed her tail and pulled until the rope was taut. One of the servants swung an axe, but the blow glanced off the cow's forehead. As she staggered, the rope snapped and she and the boy were carried away on the west wind. They were blown to safety in an uncharted jungle.

From this one cow sprang other cows, until the boy had two hundred head of cattle. Each day he drove them to a different pasture to graze, and each afternoon he took them to the river to drink. Once his cows were fed and watered and penned for the night, the boy bathed in the river and washed his hair.

One evening a hair from his head fell out and was swept downstream. A princess who had come to the river to bathe found it and took it home with her. Never before had she seen a strand of hair so long — it was as long as she was tall — or as beautiful. It was like strong, black, silk thread. Showing it to her father, she declared, "I've made up my mind to marry the man to whom this hair belongs."

The king knew there was no gainsaying his daughter once she got an idea in her head, so he sent for the royal barber. "My daughter wishes to marry the man with hair as long as she is tall. Find him for me."

After several weeks the barber returned empty-handed.

"I cut the hair and trim the beards of most men in this kingdom, but I do not know this man and I cannot find him," he said apologetically.

The king knew his daughter — she would not rest until this wretched boy was found — so he instructed his parrot to search

for the man with hair as long as the princess was tall. After only a few hours, the parrot spotted the boy from the air. He was washing his hair in the river, his flute hanging in a bush at his side. The parrot seized the flute in her beak and flew off with it, alighting on a small bush a little further on. The boy, anxious not to lose his flute, followed her. But each time he got within arm's length of her, she flew on ahead, from bush to bush, until she had lured him up to the palace gates.

On seeing the boy, the king's servants rushed him inside and measured his hair. "It must be as long as the princess is tall! Fetch her, quickly!" they cried.

When the princess was brought into the throne room carrying the treasured hair that she had found in the river, it was clear that it belonged to the same young man.

"So this is the man," said the king. "Eat and drink as much as you like. The day after tomorrow, you will marry my daughter."

"But I must return to look after my cattle first," said the boy.

"Stay the night and fetch them tomorrow," said the king.

It was quite late the next morning when the boy set out to fetch his cattle, and it was noon before he found them. Angry at being penned in without food and water for most of the morning, they knocked him down as he opened the gate and trampled on him, tearing his hair out. Battered and bruised, he sat up and found to his horror that he was completely bald. Undaunted, he rounded up the belligerent cattle and started his return journey to the king's palace. As he drove them along, the cattle melted away one by one into the jungle, so that by the time he arrived at the palace, he had lost his cattle as well as his hair.

The king barely recognized the young man who appeared in his throne room. As for the princess, it was the hair she had loved, not the man, so the marriage was off as far as she was concerned.

"I'm sorry," said the king. "My daughter no longer wants you, so you cannot be my son-in-law. You don't have any cattle left, so you cannot be my cowherd. The best I can do is apprentice you to my barber, for no one will know the value of a fine head of hair better than you."

The Tiger and the Cat

IN THE BEGINNING, tigers were the stupidest of all creatures. They didn't know anything. So the king of the tigers went to the cat to ask for lessons.

The cat taught the tiger how to stalk, and crouch, and spring, and many other things. At last the tiger thought he knew it all and decided to put his new knowledge into practice. He leaped at the cat, intending to kill and eat him.

In a flash, the cat ran up a tree, where the tiger could not follow.

"Come down," roared the tiger. "Come down this minute!"

"No! No!" replied the cat. "It's just as well I didn't teach you everything I know. Otherwise, you would be able to fetch me down yourself."

And that is why the tiger cannot climb trees.

The Blacksmith's Daughter

King Gholam had an only son called Ghul who spent every waking hour hunting. His father hated this obsession and decided that if his son married, he might settle down and change for the better. So Gholam called all his councillors together and told them to find a wife for his son. But their efforts were futile — the prince ignored all the girls paraded before him and carried on hunting as before.

Each evening when the prince returned, King Gholam would say, "If you carry on like this, no one will want to marry you and you'll give yourself and your family a bad reputation."

"But I don't want to marry," Ghul would reply, and that would be that.

One hot, sultry evening, exhausted from the hunt, Ghul stopped at a well to drink.

"Can I borrow your bowl to drink from?" he asked a girl by the well.

"Oh," she said, handing him her bowl. "Aren't you the prince whom no one will marry?"

Prince Ghul's face darkened. Dashing the bowl to the ground, he stalked off. "When I get home," he thought, "I'll tell my father I intend to marry, and I'll marry that impudent girl by the well."

A little further on he met an old woman. "Who's that girl?" he asked.

"She's Akim, the blacksmith's, daughter," the woman replied.

"I don't care who she is, I shall marry her and no one else," thought Ghul.

That evening the prince informed his astonished father that he was now prepared to marry. King Gholam called his councillors together again and told them to find a suitable wife, but Ghul stopped him short by announcing that he had already made his choice. "I'm going to marry the blacksmith's daughter."

His father was furious. "Do you seriously think you can marry someone so far beneath you? I won't allow it!"

However, the king's ministers calmed him down and persuaded him otherwise. "What harm can it do?" they said. "Let him have the girl and in the meantime we can search for someone more suitable."

So King Gholam sent his ministers to the blacksmith to ask for his daughter's hand in marriage. Akim threw up his hands in horror. "Why does the king bother to ask when he can command? But since he does ask, the answer is no, I will not let my daughter marry the prince."

Akim's answer was conveyed to the king who, blind with rage, decreed that the marriage would take place in two months' time. But the blacksmith's daughter begged for one year's grace, which was duly granted.

The blacksmith's daughter was determined to prove that she would be a good match for Ghul. But how could she gain the people's respect? She decided to test the wits of the king and his ministers and she hit on an idea. "I will make some large, unfired clay jars which I will paint and enamel," she told her father. "I'll put a watermelon in each jar, and when the fruit is fully grown, I will challenge the king, the prince, and all their ministers to remove the melons without breaking the jars. Then we shall see who is wise!"

When the melons were fully grown, she sent a letter to the king, the prince, and their ministers with two of the jars, asking them to free the melons without breaking the jars. The ministers peered into the jars, they stuck their fingers down the necks and felt the size of the melons, they scratched their heads and made endless mathematical calculations, but they couldn't work out what to do. "It's impossible!" they concluded.

So the king returned the jars, saying, "There is no one wise enough to perform this feat in the whole of my kingdom."

The girl was delighted. She sought an audience with the king and asked if she could show them how it was done. Taking a wet cloth, she wrapped it around each jar until the clay was soft and pliable. Then, stretching the necks, she pulled out the melons and reshaped the jars as before. Handing the melons to the king and his ministers, she said, "A man is recognized by his voice, a jar by its sound. If you had sounded these jars of clay, you would have discovered their true nature. By sounding you, I have found you lack common sense. I am more than your equal, so I shall marry the prince at the end of the year."

When the prince and Akim's daughter were married, he began to treat her badly. He constantly taunted and belittled her in front of friends, and sometimes struck her when he lost his temper. She bore all this with fortitude until one day, goaded beyond reason, she asked him simply, "What pleasure do you get from humiliating me? Is it because I'm a blacksmith's daughter? I bet you wouldn't dare to ill-treat a king's daughter. Try to win one, if you can!"

Prince Ghul was incensed. He vowed he would not set foot in the palace again until he had married a princess. Hearing of a princess in a nearby country who was renowned for her beauty, he set off on his best horse with ten mules laden with gold and jewels to buy his way into her heart.

On arriving in the country, he learned that the princess never spoke, and that she would only marry the man who beat her at chess. No one had succeeded. But Prince Ghul was far too arrogant to contemplate defeat. Undeterred, he sent his servant to announce his arrival and ask for the princess's hand in marriage.

"He must first understand the rules," said the king. "He will play three games of chess. If he loses the first, he loses his horse. If he loses the second, he loses his servant. If he loses the third, my daughter can make him a groom in her stables if she wishes."

The prince accepted these conditions without hesitation and the great drum was sounded to advise the townspeople that yet another suitor was trying his luck at chess.

When the prince arrived at the palace, the princess was already seated on a rich, red carpet, the chess board in front of her. They played three games and the prince lost all of them. Ten minutes later he was mucking out the horses in the palace stables.

Time flew by and the blacksmith's daughter began to wonder what had become of her husband. Disguising herself as a handsome nobleman, she set off on a beautiful horse for the kingdom of the silent princess. After many miles she reached a broad and deep river. While she was waiting for the ferry to cross, she noticed a rat being carried downstream.

"Save me! Save me!" screamed the rat. Impulsively, the blacksmith's daughter lowered her lance into the water and the rat scrambled up it to safety.

"Where are you going?" the rat asked.

"To the kingdom of the silent princess."

"Why?" asked the rat. "If you think you can beat her at chess, you're sadly mistaken. The princess owns a cat with a magic light on its head which makes it invisible. She uses the cat to mix up the pieces so that her opponents always lose."

"Since I helped you, will you help me?" she asked.

The rat peered at her through narrow eyes. "You have the hands and feet of a woman, but you dress like a man. Which are you?"

So the blacksmith's daughter told the rat her story and begged for his assistance in finding her husband, Ghul.

"One good turn deserves another," said the rat. "Take me with you, hidden up your sleeve. If you do what I tell you, you will defeat the princess and gain your heart's desire."

The next day when the blacksmith's daughter was shown in to the princess's throne room, she immediately asked if they could change places to play chess. This meant that she would be near the door through which the cat might come. Sinking into the silk cushions, she studied the chess pieces carefully. After the first few moves, she noticed that the board was becoming confused. The cat must be there! So she slipped the rat from her sleeve. There was a rush of air and an almost inaudible hiss as the cat chased after it. The blacksmith's daughter struck out in alarm and hit the magic cat. Her hand swept the light from its head, and the cat instantly became visible. The rat forgotten, the cat rushed from the room, howling, its hair on end.

The princess had never been particularly good at chess — she had always had her cat to help her — so she was easily beaten. "Checkmate," said the blacksmith's daughter for the third and final time, and a huge drum was sounded to tell the townspeople that the princess had been beaten.

But the blacksmith's daughter had not won the princess yet. To gain her hand, she had to persuade the princess, who had never been known to utter a word in her life, to speak three times before sunrise. Each time the princess spoke, the drum would be sounded to inform the king's subjects.

"We'll make this wretched woman speak!" the rat told the blacksmith's daughter, "You'll be sleeping in the same room. Let me hide under the princess's bed before you ask her to speak."

They retired to their beds, the princess on one side of the room, the blacksmith's daughter on the other. "Light of my life, beautiful princess," said the blacksmith's daughter, "will you speak to me?" The princess bit her lips and said nothing, but the rat, pretending to be the princess, replied, "Dear prince, sweet prince, I would talk forever if you asked me to."

When the princess heard this, she thought, "This man must be a magician. He can make the leg of my bed answer for me!" Shaking with fury, she shouted, "You treacherous leg! I'll hack you to pieces and throw you in the fire." The instant the words had left her mouth, the slave ran to beat the drum.

In the silence after the drum's echo had faded, the blacksmith's daughter said, "My dear princess, I long to hear your voice. Tell me a story to send me to sleep."

The rat replied, "Very well, I will tell you a story." And this is the story he told:

A robber once lived in this city, but he was so successful that he had to leave the country because he had run out of people to rob. Thinking he would not be gone long, he left his wife behind. During his absence, a thief came to the house and convinced the robber's wife that he was her missing husband.

Eventually the robber returned. Finding the thief in his house, he asked him who he was.

"Who are you?" the thief echoed.

"This is my house," the robber replied. "My wife lives here."

"How dare you!" shouted the thief. "This woman is my wife, not yours. You're a scoundrel. If you don't leave, I shall call the police!"

The robber was flabbergasted. "Wife, don't you recognize me? I'm your husband."

"Nonsense," said his wife brusquely. "I've never set eyes on you before." And with that she pushed him out of the house.

The next morning all the villagers saw the robber on the doorstep and welcomed him home. "You've made a terrible mistake," they told his wife. "This is your real husband, the other man is not." But the woman was confused. Finally she announced that her husband must be the man who could bring home the most money.

The thief asked the robber, "What do you do?"

"I'm a robber," the robber replied. "What do you do?"

"I steal," said the thief. "Let's see which of us is best at his profession. The winner will keep the woman."

"Agreed," said the robber. "You try first, since you thought of it."

The thief hired some clothes and a carriage and went to another city, where he posed as a wealthy merchant. Stopping at a jewel merchant's shop, he asked the owner if he had any pearls for sale.

"Yes," answered the merchant.

"I want to see the finest pearls you have," said the thief.

The merchant produced several strings of pearls in a box, and the thief examined them closely. "Not bad, not bad, but I'm looking for pearls that are flawless. Do you have have any more?"

The merchant produced several other boxes, all made of silk, one of which the thief opened. When the merchant was looking the other way, he cut off two strings and hid them up his sleeve.

"How many boxes of pearls do you have?" he asked the merchant.

"Seven in all," the merchant replied.

"I'll come back later to buy some of them," said the thief. But on leaving the merchant's shop he went straight to the palace to see the king.

"Oh, king," the thief said solemnly, "I've come to seek your help. Seven boxes of pearls were stolen from me and I've reason to believe that they are in the shop of a certain merchant. Would you help me recover them?"

The king gave the thief an escort and told him to search the merchant's shop. If the boxes were found, the merchant would be arrested.

On arriving at the shop, the thief pointed to the box from which he had stolen the pearls and told the soldiers that all of his boxes were made of silk like that one. They returned to the palace, the merchant under heavy guard.

"This is my box," said the thief.

"No, my lord, it is mine," the merchant cried.

"If it is yours," continued the thief, "you will know how many strings of pearls it contains. Tell the king."

"One hundred," said the merchant promptly.

"No, it doesn't," said the thief. "It contains ninety-eight."

"Count them!" ordered the king.

The strings of pearls were counted and the thief was, of course, correct.

"As you can see, the box must be mine — otherwise how could I have known how many strings of pearls it contained? This man must have stolen all of my other boxes too!"

"The box must indeed be yours," said the king. "We will find the others and return them to you." Then, waving his hand at the unfortunate merchant, he said, "Throw this man into prison!"

The robber, who had watched this farce in total amazement, could not begin to imagine how he could outdo such a crime.

"Now," said the rat, "you must understand that the king who handed over these priceless pearls to a swindler and a thief was none other than the father of your beloved princess."

The princess went scarlet with fury. She shook her fist at the offending bed leg. "I'll have you smashed to smithereens and hurled in the fire, you lying traitor!"

Her words were almost drowned out by the heavy beat of the great drum as the servant signalled for the second time that the princess had spoken.

"Beautiful princess," said the blacksmith's daughter, "I enjoyed your story. Please, would you tell me another?"

And the rat answered, "I'll tell you the robber's story, if you like."

The next day the robber said, "Now it's my turn. But before we set out, you must promise not to say a word, no matter what happens, otherwise you lose."

The thief agreed to remain silent, whatever the provocation.

The robber decided that he could not outdo the thief. Instead he must somehow contrive to discredit him. After spending some time roaming around the city listening to gossip, he learned that the king liked to sleep on the roof of his palace in hot weather, since a cool breeze came up from the river below.

"Follow me!" he said to the thief. "But remember, not a word."

By hammering iron pegs into the wall of the palace, the robber managed to climb onto the roof. The king was asleep. One soldier stood guard over him. When he turned his back, the robber leaped on him, cut his throat and threw his body into the river. Then the robber put the guard's gun to his shoulder and began to march up and down. The thief, who had followed him onto the roof, sat down in the shadows and watched.

The king stirred and cried, "Sentry!"

"Yes, sir," replied the robber smartly.

"Come over here and tell me a story. I can't sleep very well."

So the robber sat down next to the king and began to tell him the story of the thief, the jewel merchant, and the pearls. As the story unfolded, the thief frantically signalled to the robber to change the subject, but the robber ignored him.

Suddenly the robber broke off and began to tell the king his own story — of how he had scaled the palace walls and killed the sentry.

"Good lord!" exclaimed the king. "Who are you?"

"I am the robber."

"Where is my sentry, then?" asked the king.

"Lying dead in the river," replied the robber.

The king looked down and saw the truth of it.

"Finish your story," he commanded.

"But your majesty, I was telling you the story of the thief because this same thief is sitting right there!" said the robber, pointing at the thief. "The merchant is completely innocent."

The king ordered the thief to be arrested and the merchant to be released. Then he ordered that the pearls be divided equally between the robber and the merchant. The robber got half the pearls and his wife. The thief was executed.

"Now all I have to add to this charming tale," said the rat, "is that the king who rewards murderers with another man's property is the father of your beloved princess!"

The princess hurled her pillow at the bed leg.

"You'll burn too!" she screamed as the drum beat for the third and final time.

The next morning the city was buzzing, for the king had declared a public holiday so that everyone could celebrate the princess's marriage later that day. As soon as the ceremony was over, the blacksmith's daughter turned to the princess. "I followed your rules to win you, now you must follow mine. You may not set foot in my rooms for the next six months."

As the weeks went by, the sham prince became increasingly popular and famed for "his" wisdom and charm. The king deferred to his "son-in-law" in all matters of state and agreed to "his" every whim. So when the blacksmith's daughter suggested that all the unfortunate princes now working in the palace stables should be released and allowed to return to their homes, the king naturally concurred. However, since the blacksmith's daughter herself took charge of freeing the six hundred who had failed to win the princess, she was able to ensure that Ghul was not released. Instead she told him that he would be required to prepare her horse each day and accompany her on expeditions.

After some time, the "prince" went to the king and begged to be allowed to return to her own country for a short visit. The king agreed, and so the "prince" set off with the princess and Ghul, who was guarded to ensure that he did not try to escape.

Ghul soon realized that they were nearing his own country. He wondered ruefully what the blacksmith's daughter would think if she could see him like this.

They were three days' ride from the capital when they stopped for the night and the "prince" called Ghul to her. "I have urgent business to attend to, for which I need a disguise. You must change clothes with me and take my place in my absence. I have instructed my men that this is in order. Stay here a month. I will see you again soon."

The prince obeyed. But the blacksmith's daughter, dressed in the groom's clothing and carrying his currycomb and brush, went just as far as her father's house and no further.

After a couple of days, Ghul became restless.

"What's to stop me from taking the princess to my father and claiming I won her myself?" he thought.

So that night he gave orders to strike camp, and three days later he arrived triumphantly in the capital. Trumpets sounded, banners waved, and a proclamation was made in the street that Prince Ghul had won the famous silent princess.

The next day, Prince Ghul sent for the blacksmith's daughter. "Well, what have you got to say now?" he said when she appeared. "I won the famous silent princess!"

"Did you really win her or did I?" she asked quietly.

"I did!" he said.

"You lie," said the blacksmith's daughter. Then, clapping her hands, she summoned a servant bearing a box. She signalled to everyone to retire and leave the two of them alone. Then she unlocked the box and removed the currycomb, the brush, and the groom's clothes, "Whose are these?" she asked. "Yours or mine?"

Speechless, the prince looked at the shabby clothes and brushes. Then he stammered, "M-m-m-mine."

"Then who won the princess, you or I?"

"You did," he replied.

"Don't you see," said the blacksmith's daughter, "that if you and your father and your father's councillors couldn't solve the puzzle of the earthen jars, then you couldn't possibly win the silent princess? But now, take her, and marry her, if you wish. Then we can all be happy at last."

The Man Who Went to Seek his Fate

THERE HAS NEVER been a time when men have not struggled, but some men struggle more than most. Lal was such a man. This is his story.

A thin, toneless wail curdled the air. One of the children was crying again. Lal couldn't remember a time when one of them wasn't. They always cried from hunger, but now that winter had set in, they cried from the cold too.

"Oh, God! Why are you doing this to us?" Lal moaned, shaking his fist at the sky. "You bless us with twelve children, then curse us with poverty so that we can't afford to feed or clothe them. I haven't worked for twelve years, and I despair of ever finding work again. If I don't, we won't survive much longer."

Turning to his wife, he said desperately, "I've got to do something — God won't help us — so I'm going to find my fate and learn what the future holds for me."

The next morning he set off early and was in the forest by noon. He was in a very dense stretch of woodland when he saw a camel with two sacks of gold strapped to her back. The camel was lame, her coat dull and matted, and where the leather had cut in to her stomach, her skin was raw and chafed. "What are you doing here?" Lal asked.

"I once belonged to the Rajah. Our caravan was going to Lahore, carrying gold for the princess's dowry. Each night we stopped as the light faded, and we struck camp again at dawn.

One morning the servants forgot me and I couldn't remember the way to Lahore or the way home. I have been wandering around this forest for twelve years with these bags strapped to my back. But where are you going?"

"I am going to find my fate to ask it why I'm so poor," replied Lal.

"Would you ask it for me why I've been wandering around this forest for twelve years with these sacks on my back and whether I'll ever be free of them?" asked the camel.

"Of course I will," said Lal. "If you stay near here, I'll give you the answer on my way home. Now, if you'll excuse me, I've got a long way to go." Patting the camel's shoulder, he set off again.

The forest soon began to thin and the ground dropped away into a deep ravine with a river rushing through it. The river was infested with crocodiles, and Lal was standing on the bank wondering how to get across when one of them asked, "Where are you going?"

"To seek my fate and ask it why I'm so poor," said Lal.

"If I take you across the river, will you ask it why I've had a fire in my belly for the past twelve years?" asked the crocodile.

"It's a deal," replied Lal, climbing on to the crocodile's back.

In the mid-afternoon, Lal saw a tiger lying in the shade of a banyan tree, licking his paw. A huge thorn stuck out of his foot just below one of his claws.

"Where are you off to?" the tiger yawned.

"I'm going to ask my fate why I'm so poor," Lal replied. "Someone once told me that I should look for my stone of fate, and if it was lying down, I should beat it with a stick."

"Would you do something for me?" asked the tiger. "Would you ask it why I've had this thorn in my foot for the past twelve years? I've tried to get it out, but I haven't been able to."

"Very well," answered Lal.

He walked on for twelve more days. On the morning of the thirteenth, he came to the place where everyone's fate lives. There were stones everywhere, some standing, some lying down, too numerous to count.

Lal found a heap of stones lying on the ground. "I bet that's my fate right at the bottom, buried under all the others," he muttered, "and that's why I'm so poor." And pulling a stone from the bottom of the pile, he began to hit it with his walking stick. Again and again he hit the stone, venting all the anger, frustration, and despair of the past twelve years. He beat the stone until night began to fall. Then, arms shaking, legs weak, he sank to the ground, exhausted. It was only then that God sent a soul into Lal's fate and it became a man.

"Why have you been beating me?" the fate asked Lal.

"Because you were lying down. Because I haven't had a job for twelve years. Because I am destitute, and because my wife and children are starving," Lal replied.

"I promise you will flourish from now on," the fate proclaimed.

Lal was inclined to believe him. Flooded with relief and gratitude, he inquired haltingly, "Do you mind if I ask you three questions?"

"Not at all," the fate replied.

"On the way here I met a camel who's been wandering around with two sacks of gold strapped to her back for the last twelve years. She wants to know how to get rid of them."

"That's easy," said the fate. "When you see her again, just take the sacks off her back and she will be free."

"Of course!" exclaimed Lal. "Why didn't I think of that? Well, then I met a crocodile who's had indigestion for the last twelve years and wants to know why."

"Ask him if he remembers swallowing a ruby twelve years ago, because that's what's causing his stomachache. If he brings up the ruby, he'll feel better," the fate replied.

"I'll tell him that," said Lal. "Next I met a tiger with a thorn in his foot which he's tried to get out for the past twelve years without success."

"Just pull it out with your teeth," said the fate.

Having answered all Lal's questions, God snatched the fate's soul back. Where the man had stood, there was now a stone.

Lal nodded with satisfaction and began his homeward journey. When he met the tiger, it asked, "What did your fate say?"

"Give me your paw," Lal commanded, and bending down, he pulled the thorn out with his teeth.

"I must repay you for your kindness," said the tiger. "Follow me and I'll give you some money."

"How could you possibly have any money?" Lal asked in surprise.

"I've eaten a lot of people in my time, and I've kept all their money," said the tiger as he led Lal into his den. "Give me your headcloth and I'll fill it for you."

Lal laid his headcloth on the ground and the tiger filled it with jewels and gold coins. Then, tying the cloth to his walking stick, Lal slung it over his shoulder, thanked the tiger, and set off again.

Next he met the crocodile who had helped him cross the river.

"Did you ask your fate why my stomach burns?" asked the crocodile.

"Yes, I did," replied Lal. "You've got a ruby in your stomach and it's giving you indigestion. If you throw it up, you'll feel fine."

The crocodile opened his fearsome jaws and retched. The ruby shot out of his mouth. "Good grief!" said the crocodile. "I swallowed that years ago. Ooohh, I feel so much better. Why don't you keep the ruby, with my thanks."

Lal thanked the crocodile and set off to find the camel.

"Did you ask your fate what I should do with this burden?" asked the camel eagerly when she saw Lal.

"Yes. This!" said Lal, taking the sacks off the camel's back.

"What a relief!" exclaimed the camel. "Now I'll be able to eat and drink and sleep in comfort. In return for your kindness, I'll give you the sacks of gold. What's more, I'll carry them home for you."

When Lal arrived home with a camel laden with gold and jewels, his family was astonished and begged to be told how he'd come by these riches. Lal first let the camel go, then sat down and described his adventures in detail.

However, when a nosy villager, jealous of Lal's newfound wealth, asked him how he'd come by his riches, Lal replied, "I just threw my bucket in the river and each time I pulled it out, there was gold in the water."

The man immediately went down to the river and began to draw up bucket after bucket.

"Hey! What do you think you're doing?" shouted a crocodile. "If you keep on taking water out of the river, my fish will die!"

"I want some money, so I'll keep on taking water out of the river until I find some," replied the man.

"If you stop that at once, I'll give you money," said the crocodile, lashing his tail. A huge arc of water curled onto the bank, bringing with it a pile of gold coins. The man filled his bucket and went home. The following morning he was back again, greedy for more, and the next day and the day after that.

Eventually the crocodile lost patience and swallowed the man whole.

The man lived in the crocodile's belly for four days and four nights. On the fifth morning, the crocodile said, "I'll let you go if you promise not to tell anyone what happened to you. If you utter one word, you will end up worse than before." The man gave his word and the crocodile released him.

But on reaching home, the man just couldn't keep quiet. He said to his wife, "You'll never believe what happened to me . . ." and he told her the whole story. And from that moment on, nothing ever went right for him again.

About the Stories

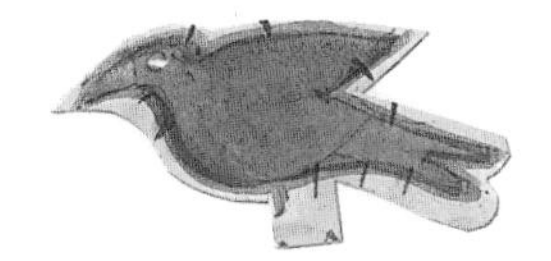

The Cat Who Became a Queen

This delightful story comes from the Rev. J. Hinton Knowles's *Folk-Tales of Kashmir* (London: Trübner & Co., 1888). Knowles was one of a number of nineteenth-century missionaries who recognized the importance of India's oral storytelling tradition, and he sought to record it faithfully. This tale was contributed to his book by Pandit Anand Kol, who collected it from a Hindu student named Rází, living in Srínagar. Shiva, the Hindu god of creation and destruction, is thought to live on Mount Kailasa in the Himalayas. Parvati, his wife, an aspect of the great goddess Devi, is known as "daughter of the mountain." Kashmir is now a disputed territory between India, Pakistan, and China.

Kanai the Gardener

From William McCulloch's *Bengali Household Tales* (London: Hodder & Stoughton, 1912). McCulloch collected his stories in verbatim shorthand during the late 1880s, mostly from "a very intelligent young Brahman, and orthodox Hindu, whose home was in an extremely out-of-the-way village, and who, when I first became acquainted with him, had been little in contact with Europeans. He possessed fine gifts, both as a talker and a *raconteur*. Yet I found no reason to doubt his oft-repeated assertion that he told me the stories exactly as he heard them." This story, in which Kanai hitches a ride up to heaven with the god Indra's elephant, Airavata (here, Oirabot), is a homely village reworking of a tale in Somadeva's original *Ocean of Story*, in which the means of ascent is the bull of Shiva; flying elephants are reasonably common in Indian folklore.

The Wind and the Sun

From *Folklore of the Santal Parganas* by Cecil Henry Bompas (London: David Nutt, 1909). The stories in this important book were collected by the Rev. O. Bodding of the Scandinavian Mission to the Santals, a Munda tribe of the Chutia Nagpore plateau, south of Bengal. The contest of the wind and the sun is well known as one of Aesop's fables, and is also found in oral traditions, especially of Eastern and Northern Europe; an African-American variant is "Brer Rabbit Treats the Creeturs to a Race" in Joel Chandler Harris's *Uncle Remus and Brer Rabbit.*

THE KING AND HIS DAUGHTERS

This little story from the Punjab will remind many readers of Shakespeare's *King Lear*; anyone intrigued by the resemblance should turn to Alan Dundes's essay "'To Love My Father All': A Psychoanalytic Study of the Folktale Source of King Lear" in his *Cinderella: A Folklore Casebook*. The "love like salt" motif is often only the opening act of a Cinderella story (such as the Italian "La Sendraoeula" in Neil Philip's *The Cinderella Story*). This version comes from Charles Swynnerton's *Indian Nights' Entertainment* (London: Archibald Constable & Co., 1892).

THE MAGIC LAMP

Another Santal story, this time collected by the Rev. A. Campbell of the Free Church of Scotland Santal Mission and published in his *Santal Folk Tales* (Pokhuria: Santal Mission Press, 1891). It is a popular treatment of the Aladdin story, which is common as an oral folktale in India. Interestingly, "Aladdin" was added to the *Arabian Nights* by the Frenchman, Antoine Galland, who produced the first Western translation in 1704; it is not in any of the manuscript sources, and Galland evidently collected it from a Maronite storyteller.

A LIKELY STORY!

This lying contest comes from Andrew Lang's *The Olive Fairy Book* (London: Longmans, Green, & Co., 1907); it was sent to him by Major Campbell of Firozpûr.

THE BOY WHO HAD A MOON ON HIS FOREHEAD AND A STAR ON HIS CHIN

From Maive Stokes's *Indian Fairy Tales* (Calcutta: Privately Printed, 1879); told by Múniyá, a Bengali *ayah* or nursemaid. In the original, a cow swallows the young prince after Shankar's death, in turn passing on the responsibility to Katar, who is described as "a fairy-horse". There is also a subplot in which the prince tricks his six brothers-in-law into letting him brand them with the mark of a thief, and then exposes them to the king. The story is a highly individual variant of the international folktale known as "The Three Golden Sons." Often the mother of the prince or princes is accused of having given birth to an animal; here, a stone. The swallowing and regurgitation by the helpful animals is unusual.

THE BRAHMAN'S LUCK

From McCulloch's *Bengali Household Tales*. Hindu folktales are full of instances of the inevitability of fate, but this is a particularly amusing example.

THE THIRSTY FOOL

This little tale, which shows how luck is of no use to someone who fails to recognize it, is part of a long sequence of stories within Somadeva's *Kathá Sarit Ságara*, translated by C. H. Tawney and edited in ten volumes as *The Ocean of Story* by N. M. Penzer (London: Privately Printed, 1924–1928).

About the Stories

THE WONDERFUL RING

This story is a tale type known to folklorists as "The Magic Ring," of which 72 variants have been collected in Greece alone. On the basis of the curious incident of the rat's tail up the nose, Joseph Jacobs argued that "there can be little doubt of the Indian origin." Among numerous other Indian versions is "The Charmed Ring" in Knowles's *Folk-Tales of Kashmir*. This version is from Flora Annie Steele's *Tales of the Punjab* (London & New York: Macmillan & Co., 1894), and was collected by Sir Richard Carnac Temple from a small boy at Firozpûr. In the original, the prince must "make a clean holy square place on the ground, plaster it over according to the custom of holy places, put the ring in the centre, [and] sprinkle it with buttermilk," before making a wish. The Punjab was divided between India and Pakistan in 1947; Firozpûr lies just on the Indian side of the border.

THREE FUSSY MEN

This tale of three Hindu brothers who are so over-delicate about their own circumstances that they forget the duty they owe their father – and yet benefit from it – was written down in *The Ocean of Story* around seven hundred years before Hans Christian Andersen immortalized this kind of tale in "The Princess and the Pea," one of the first four fairy tales he published in 1835. Andersen had heard it as a child in Denmark, and similar tales have been collected in Sweden. *The Ocean of Story* also contains the story of "King Dharmadhvaja and his Three Very Sensitive Wives": one of these is wounded by a lotus blossom, one is burned by the rays of the moon, and one is bruised all over by the sound of a pestle pounding rice in a distant house.

THE MOUSE–GIRL

The *Ocean of Story* incorporates the separate collection of tales known as the *Panchatantra*, from which this little fable comes. Whereas in "The Wind and the Sun" the elements vied as to who was the strongest, here, faced with marriage to the poor mouse-maiden, they seem only too willing to protest their weakness.

THE BRAHMAN, THE TIGER, AND THE SIX JUDGES

This fable was part of the story repertoire of Anna Liberata de Souza, an *ayah*, recorded by Mary Frere in her book *Old Deccan Days, or, Hindoo Fairy Legends Current in South India* (London: John Murray, 1868). The storyteller, although of Hindu origin, came from a Lingaet family from Goa who had been Christian for three generations; she learned her stories from her grandmother. This tale, known to folklorists as "The Ungrateful Serpent Returned to Captivity," is widely distributed across the world, with 36 recorded Indian versions, 49 African, 76 Irish, and so on. It appears both in Aesop's *Fables* and in Joel Chandler Harris's *Nights with Uncle Remus*. In India, the freed animal is a tiger; in Europe, a serpent; in Egypt, a crocodile.

THE PRINCE WHO WAS CHANGED INTO A RAM

This story was collected by J. Hinton Knowles from Shiva Báyú of Renawárí, Srínagar, and published in *Folk-Tales of Kashmir*. The original contains an interesting but gruesome incident on the prince and princess's flight. They are attacked by the son of a jinn, an evil creature "with only half a body," and the prince is killed. The princess promises to marry the half-man, but tricks it and kills it, whereupon the prince is restored to life by a holy man.

THE BOY AND HIS STEPMOTHER

This tale from Campbell's *Santal Folk Tales* offers a cynical twist on the Cinderella theme. Another Santal version, which also ends on a note of disappointment, though not so sadly as this one, is "How the Cowherd Found a Bride" in Bompas's *Folklore of the Santal Parganas*. "The Golden Hair" from P. K. Mitra and Rai Bahadur *Mundari Folk Tales* and "The Story of the Black Cow" in Alice Elizabeth Dracott's *Simla Village Tales* are similar, but end well. The Zuñi Cinderella, "Poor Turkey Girl" (in Frank Hamilton Cushing's *Zuñi Folk Tales* and also Philip's *The Cinderella Story*), has a comparable unhappy ending. The motif of the search for a spouse through a randomly cast hair can be found in one of the earliest recorded folktales, the Egyptian "Anpu and Bata," preserved in a papyrus dating from about 1250 BC.

THE TIGER AND THE CAT

As "The Fox and the Cat" this fable appears both in Aesop and Grimm: the fox has a hundred tricks, and the cat only one, climbing trees. The cat escapes from the hunt with its one trick, but the fox is captured. This version comes from Swynnerton's *Indian Nights' Entertainment*.

THE BLACKSMITH'S DAUGHTER

This tale bears a close resemblance to the story of Patient Griselda, which was very popular in medieval Europe, appearing in both Boccaccio's *Decameron* and Chaucer's *Canterbury Tales*, and later versified by Charles Perrault. But unlike the European Griselda, the Indian wife is not content to submit to her husband's cruelty. She stands up to him, and, in fact, makes a fool of him. This particular story type is found only in India, and is known as "The Wife Who Would Not Be Beaten," which is the title of the version in Bompas's *Folklore of the Santal Parganas*; eleven Indian variants have been recorded. This version was told by Hâji Shah in November 1879 and published in Swynnerton's *Indian Nights' Entertainment*. Swynnerton collected his tales mostly from professional Muslim storytellers on the Upper Indus, in what is now Pakistan.

THE MAN WHO WENT TO SEEK HIS FATE

From *Indian Fairy Tales* by Maive Stokes; told by Dunkní. The story of the poor man's journey in search of fortune, a tale type in itself, offers another point of view on the inevitability of fate. The story bears some resemblance to the more elaborate European fairy tale of "Three Hairs from the Devil's Beard," familiar from Grimm.

FURTHER READING

The best introduction to India's storytelling traditions is *Folktales of India* edited by Brenda E. F. Beck and others (Chicago & London: University of Chicago Press, 1987). Joseph Jacobs's *Indian Fairy Tales* (London: David Nutt, 1892) is still in print; although retold for children, it is a sound collection with useful notes. Three key reference books are Jawaharlal Handoo's *A Bibliography of Indian Folk Literature* (Mysore: Central Institute of Indian Languages, 1977), Stith Thompson and Jonas Balys's *The Oral Tales of India* (Bloomington: Indiana University Press, 1958), and Stith Thompson and Warren E. Roberts's *Types of Indic Oral Tales* (Helsinki: Suomalainen Tiedeakatemia, 1960; with a supplement by Heda Jason, 1989).

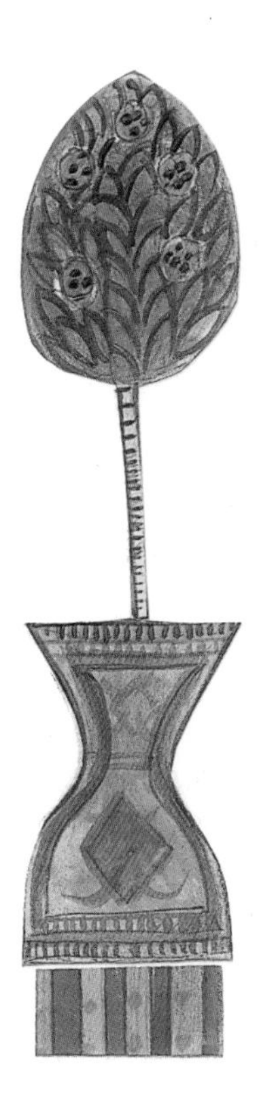